BLUEFISHING

Also by Henry Lyman:

BOTTOM FISHING (with Frank Woolner)
STRIPED BASS FISHING (with Frank Woolner)

BLUEFISHING
HENRY LYMAN

Nick Lyons Books

Printed in the United States of America

10 9 8 7 6 5 4 3 2 1

Portions of this book have appeared previously in *Successful Bluefishing* by the same author.

Library of Congress Cataloging-in-Publication Data

Lyman, Henry, 1915–
  Bluefishing.

  Includes index.
  1. Bluefishing. I. Title.
SH691.B55L918   1987   799.1'758   87–18487
ISBN 0–941130–57–6
ISBN 0–941130–58–4 (pbk.)

CONTENTS

PREFACE

An old jingle, giving advice on what a new bride should wear, runs: "Something old, something new, something borrowed, something blue." It is an apt description of this book. Back in 1950, I wrote my first volume about bluefish. It was rewritten and revised twice, with the latest edition appearing in 1974. This present effort contains much of the old information previously included. However, new information on the fish, tackle and methods of catching has been added.

As far as borrowing is concerned, I have unashamedly taken material from others who have written on the same subject as well as from countless fishermen with whom I have talked when afloat or ashore. Many of them I have never known by name and can only hope that they will recognize their contributions. These appear with my heartfelt thanks. The "blue" I trust is self-evident.

This is my terminal book on bluefish. I am not being morbid when I write this: I am merely stating a fact. Having passed the Biblical limit of three score years and ten, I know my own limitations. Although those who are not authors may not realize it, it is far more difficult to produce deathless prose on a subject covered rather thoroughly over a long period of years than it is to write on an entirely new topic. If I ever have the opportunity to fish for Nile perch, for example, I might well be persuaded to pen a splendid dissertation on the species. Concerning bluefish, however, I must rest content with all that follows.

Particular thanks are due to those on the staff of *Salt Water Sportsman* magazine. Those who have taken over the periodical were kind enough to give me the title of Publisher Emeritus and to allow me to remain in the office where I can pound out copy according to my own time schedule. Fishermen all, they have contributed much of their own knowledge on the latest developments on the bluefishing front, have picked well-rounded holes in some of my pet theories, and have allowed me to pore over their amazing collection of photographs for use in this book.

The rollcall includes Frank Woolner—friend, fisherman, hunter, military historian, a true naturalist in the old sense of the word. As Senior Editor, he has collaborated with me in the writing of many books and articles over the years. E.F. "Spider" Andresen, Publisher, and C.M. "Rip" Cunningham, Editor-in-Chief, not only have provided information, but also have guided me to red-hot bluefishing grounds of the islands of Nantucket an Martha's Vineyard. Editor Barry Gibson, a charter skipper in his own right, has kept me up to date particularly concerning the tastes and whims of bluefish around his base of operations in Boothbay Harbor, Maine. His wife Jean has produced many of the sketches which appear in the following pages. Associate Editor Whit Griswold is a bearcat on detail and definitions, which has assisted me greatly in my vague and wordy ramblings. Finally Regional Editor Al Ristori has answered many of my questions concerning the New York–New Jersey area with which he is most familiar.

In the scientific world, the late Dr. Lionel A. Walford not only provided me with much unpublished material on the life habits of bluefish while he was Director of the Sandy Hook Marine Laboratory in Highlands, New Jersey, but also steered me to many other scientists working in the field. Their contributions, written and verbal, provided facts that otherwise would have been pure conjecture.

As always, Nick Lyons, Peter Burford and their able staff have given sound advice on all phases of publishing this book. Finally, my wife Marjorie has been most understanding as a fishing widow who also understands the meaning of editorial deadlines.

HENRY LYMAN
Cambridge, Massachusetts

1

The Fish

Slashing, snapping, driving frantic bait fish before them in showers of silver, bluefish move through many of the warmer seas of the world as efficient killers—predators supreme. Streamlined, ferocious, often canibalistic, they are a match for any fish of their own size and more than a match for most. They are in a class by themselves.

Scientists have recognized this fact. They have placed the species in the family *Pomatomidae* and it is the only member of that family known today. The bluefish's official title of *Pomatomus saltatrix* may be translated as "a sheathed, leaping, cutting edge." The name is apt, as many fishermen, bearing scars from the needle-sharp teeth of a biting bluefish know to their cost.

Little was known about the life cycle of the species until comparatively recently. The great naturalist Louis Agassiz thought he had discovered fertilized eggs in the 1860's, hatched them carefully—and ended up with a jar full of silver hake fry! Later, he evidently did isolate free floating eggs, but his hatching experiments resulted in failure. Larvae captured by Agassiz and several other marine scientists during the following three decades were identified and described as young bluefish. These descriptions varied considerably and the researchers in some cases obviously were working with another species.

It was not until 1959 that Soviet scientist L.P. Salekhova managed to hatch eggs from ripe roe and milt obtained from spawning blues in the Black Sea. She kept them alive for five days and published the first undeniably accurate description known. A couple of years later, similar hatching experiments conducted at the Sandy Hook Marine Laboratory in New Jersey kept specimens alive even longer, further corroborating what a bluefish looks like in infancy.

For those who like their bluefish very small, the outstanding characteristics after they start to look more like a fish than an embryo are dark blue eyes, easily distinguishable dorsal fins, and the start of those death-dealing teeth. Some years ago, I managed to dredge up some of them in a plankton net haul along the shores of Nomans Land off the coast of Massachusetts.

I have observed the spawning behavior of bluefish in inshore waters thanks to the late Winslow Warren of Massachusetts and the late Captain Warren H. Whitehead of North Carolina. When I wrote in the 1950's that no one had discovered spawning grounds of the species in the Atlantic, I was informed in a polite way by this angling pair that I was a liar. They had both observed blues multiplying their kind along the southern shore of Nomans Land and they took me on several trips to watch the event. In addition, several readers of *Salt Water Sportsman* magazine during this same period described similar activity in the Coney Island area off New York and in the eastern part of Boston Harbor.

Female fish swim slowly along in water usually less than ten feet in depth. They are escorted by several males trailing astern, but I have yet to see more than four males following one of the opposite sex. The female rolls on her side and extrudes eggs while the males, rolling at a far more rapid rate, fertilize them. There is no bunting of the female, as is common among some other marine species. I have never been able to hook a fish engaged in spawning.

Even before spawning, blues are difficult to catch. They seem to prefer at that time a spoon or metal jig, although they will also take an underwater plug and, rarely, a surface lure or fly. My guess is that they attack to protect their territory rather than to obtain food. It would be chivalric to think that the males alone did the attacking in defense of their lady love, but such is not the case. I and others have caught fish of both sexes under these conditions. After spawning, blues are ravenous and will usually hit anything offered to them.

As will be noted later, blues spawn offshore as well as inshore. The known inshore grounds all have similar characteristics: fairly shallow water, broken and rocky bottom, and a sharp drop-off facing the open sea.

In 1960, a modest research effort on bluefish was mounted at the Sandy Hook Marine Laboratory. The original laboratory burned down in 1985, but work still continues under the aegis of the National Marine Fisheries Service. Although the 1960 project started in a small way, it rapidly developed into a coastwide program along the Atlantic Coast from New England to Florida. For much of the material that follows, I am indebted to the many researchers who have worked in cooperation with that laboratory's staff.

Once a baby blue has reached the size at which it can be readily identified, it starts to eat at an extraordinary rate of speed. Snappers, which are young fish weighing less than a pound, jump from eight inches and a half-pound to almost 14 inches and better than two pounds in a single year. Weight is nearly doubled in the third year, and a four-year-old weighs on the average more than six pounds and measures approximately 21 inches.

It should be noted at this point that bluefish between a pound and two pounds in many areas are called tailors, or tailor blues. In some sections of Chesapeake Bay in former days, any bluefish was so termed. Just to confuse things further, Australians call *all* bluefish tailors. If you move to South Africa, the name is elf and, in Argentina, salmon argentino. In the United States, there are various local titles, such as "Hatteras blues" designating specimens taken off the cape of that name in North Carolina when they weigh five pounds or better. Some Rhode Islanders label snappers as skipjack and, off the Maryland and Virginia coasts, "summer blues" is not the name of a song, but fish of two to three pounds.

American anglers are imaginative and are always dreaming up new terms. "Chopper" has been a bluefish nickname since the early days of angling literature in this country. The reason is obvious: just watch those bluefish jaws at work! "Slammers" and "jumbos" to designate exceptionally large specimens made their linguistic appearance when the runs of big fish came in the 1960's. Undoubtedly other names will develop in future years. Some may drop from common usage, just as the old terms "snapping mackerel" and "greenfish" have.

Returning to the growth rate, increases slow down appreciably after the blue's sixth birthday, at which time individuals weigh

Average length and weight of bluefish at ages one through fourteen. National Marine Fisheries Service.

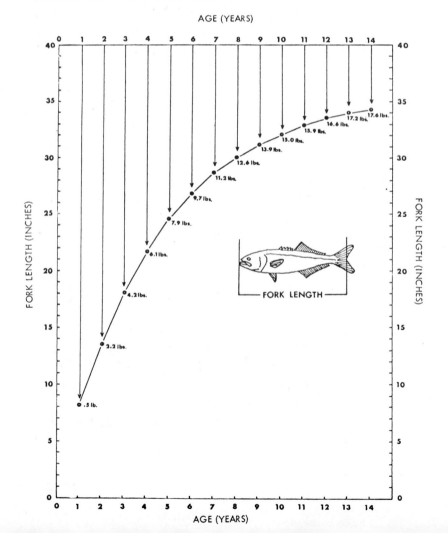

James Hussey holding his 31-pound, 12-ounce bluefish caught off Hatteras Inlet on the Outer Banks of North Carolina. He made the catch on a plastic eel and 30-pound-test line. The fish shattered a 19-year-old record for the largest bluefish according to the IGFA.

almost ten pounds. This slow-down is typical of many marine species. A 15-pounder is about ten years old and a 17½-pounder, about 14. Just how old the present International Game Fish Association (IGFA) record fish of 31 pounds, 12 ounces, was is anyone's guess. This monster was taken on January 30, 1972, by James M. Hussey of Tarboro, North Carolina, and measured 46½ inches. The fish, caught off Hatteras Inlet, displaced the previous record of 24 pounds, 3 ounces, hooked in 1952 off the Azores.

Before leaving Hussey's huge fish, it should also be noted that such specimens may well be considered giants of their kind rather than exceptionally large, normal bluefish. Anglers tend to believe that very large individual game fish of any kind are large simply because they are very old. Rarely is this the case. As a fish ages, it must spend more time catching enough food to sustain itself. Growth rate slows down and, in extreme cases, very old fish actually lose weight in their declining years. It may well be that this record blue, which is believed to have been about 20 years old, had some sort of glandular abnormality which caused it to reach such a size.

I have seen some equivalent monsters off the North African Coast taken by local commercial fishermen, who normally drift a live bait on a handline; then, when the blue has been hooked, let it fight a light dhow—a locally made small boat—by snubbing the line around a cleat until the fish is exhausted. Phil Mayer of New York City reported to me that he saw a 45-pounder taken in this manner. This appears to be about maximum weight for the species.

Up until the middle of the last century, many fishermen believed sincerely that snapper blues were a completely different species than their adult brethren. The younger fish with large heads and small bodies, and adults with these characteristics reversed, gave rise to this theory. In addition, the appearance of the two age groups at widely different times of year on many sections of the coasts supported the myth. Marine biologists long since have exploded this particular fantasy, but there certainly is some question about the different populations, or races, of blues. Here, things become complicated.

Taxonomists apparently enjoy dividing species into sub-species and giving each group a different name. I deplore this muddying of the classification waters and will try to outline the general habits of the distinct races, their life cycles and characteristics. Some may think that I have over-simplified.

A Sandy Hook research team spent about a half-hour per fish taking all sorts of measurements on the bluefish year classes of 1962 and 1968. The samples hatched in those two years totaled several hundred specimens. These measurements were cranked into a computer and, when the final calculations were completed, it appeared that one race, called the "northern summer spawners" for ease of reference, basically have smaller heads than another, labeled the "southern spring spawners." Remember these two races, for I plan to refer to them many times.

The southern spring spawning race apparently procreates from early spring into June at the edge of the Gulf Stream. The young then drift north under the influence of the Gulf Stream current and are carried past Cape Hatteras up towards New England. On this northbound trip, schools peel off from the main body of fish and travel westward to show up as snappers in the areas from New Jersey to southern Maine. By fall, the fish of the two races are of different sizes, with those of the spring spawners naturally being much larger than those of the northern summer spawners. Obviously they have a time advantage during which they eat as only bluefish can.

It appears that the southern-spawned fish then move south via an offshore route as the waters cool. In 1978, commercial fishermen reported an unprecedented number of bluefish of all sizes along the western edge of Georges Bank off Massachusetts from midsummer well into the autumn. During that year, water temperatures inshore were unusually cool and migrations may well have been affected by this factor. The southern spawners contribute to the winter fishery in Florida. The next year, they head north again and appear all along the coast, concentrating in New England, New York and New Jersey in particular as the season progresses. As this race grows in age and size, these blues seem to show up less and less in inshore catches. It may well be that they are basically oceanic in nature and, since there is no concentrated effort to catch them well at sea by either commercial or sport fishermen, they may live an untroubled life until dying of old age. Possibly some of them cross the Atlantic to contribute to the stocks of huge fish found off the west coast of Africa and nearby islands. This, however, has yet to be proved.

The progeny resulting from the summer spawning move southward past Cape Hatteras and evidently spend their first winter offshore. The following spring, they move into estuarine waters—primarily the sounds of North Carolina—where they remain until fall. These sounds provide excellent nurseries and it is obvious that their preservation is of primary concern for the

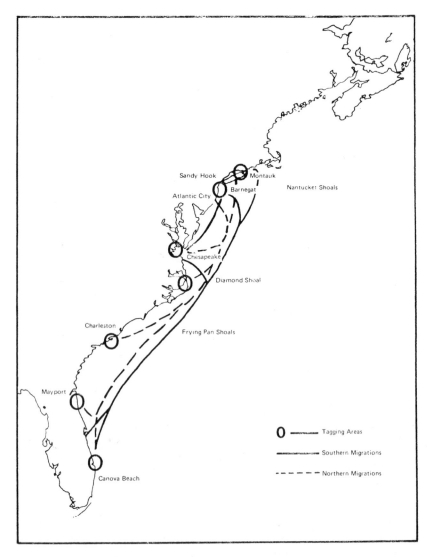

Bluefish migrations along the east coast of the United States. National Marine Fisheries Service.

future of both races of bluefish. From their second season onward, the northerners apparently follow in general a south-to-north route in the spring and summer, then a north-to-south path in the fall. Just how far offshore they move and how far south they go is still a matter for conjecture.

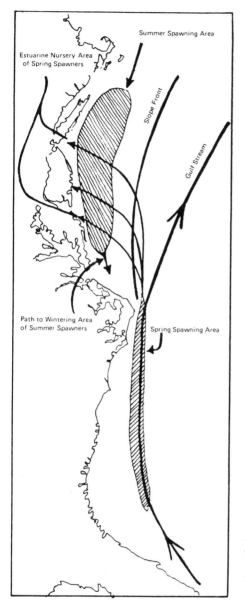

Movements of bluefish during their early life along the east coast of the United States. National Marine Fisheries Service.

Northern summer spawners make up the bulk of the bluefish that spawn close to the coast. They reproduce first in the early summer and may continue to spawn well into August. It is common knowledge that blues appear in the northern part of their range as early as May in some years, are fat and fussy in their feeding when they first arrive, then apparently vanish from many areas for a couple of weeks, only to reappear again, gaunt, hungry and mean, in midsummer. Some of their spawning grounds are known as noted, but many remain to be discovered along much of the northeast coast.

The relative number of northern- and southern-spawned blues varies from year to year. This undoubtedly reflects differences in infant mortality resulting from vagaries of water temperatures, currents and available food at the respective times and areas of their hatching. Attacks by predators and parasites may contribute to the fluctuations.

Since the major work undertaken at the Sandy Hook Laboratory, more scattered research on the species has been conducted. Preliminary findings indicate that there may well be another race, which spawns on the coast of Latin America. Indications are that at least some of these fish swim across the Gulf of Mexico and contribute to the supply of adult fish found along the Gulf shores of Florida, Alabama, Mississippi, Louisiana and Texas.

Racer bluefish, typical of the slim fish which arrive along the coasts after spawning. Photo by Frank Woolner.

Although tagging of blues has produced some knowledge of their migrations, there is still more work to be done before all the answers are supplied. Tagging itself presents a problem. In years gone by, I tagged specimens with Petersen disc-type markers—two circular bits of plastic held together by a pin thrust through the flesh of the fish. Such a tag evidently looks good to eat and the decorated blues were attacked by their fellows when returned to the water. Petersen discs are normally placed just behind the dorsal fin, so an attack on the tag meant serious injury to the fish. Today tags are usually of the spaghetti streamer type, but there may still be some mortality from their use.

That tagging is a shock to individual fish is evident from study of the scales. Adult bluefish add an annulus mark on their scales every year, much as a tree adds rings on a cross-section of its trunk. When a fish is tagged, a false annulus appears. Humans often grow a ridge on their fingernails after a particularly violent or emotional disturbance. Bluefish apparently feel the same way about being tagged.

Although studies to date explain migrations of two major races of western Atlantic Ocean bluefish, explanations of some of their movements both in that area and elsewhere around the world are still something of a mystery. For example, in the period from about 1850 through 1875 the fish were plentiful north of Boston, Massachusetts, and even reached waters off Mount Desert Island in Maine, with some strays reported from Nova Scotia. By 1879, bluefish off the coast of Maine were rare. It was almost 100 years later before the species returned to Maine's water in quantity and as this is written in 1987, blues support a considerable sport fishery in the Muscongus Bay area with some fish again as far east as Mount Desert. When blues appeared in 1973 in Nova Scotia waters after their long absence, fishermen did not know the species and thought they were a type of pollock until those bluefish teeth fastened on a few human fingers!

It is probable that an increase in sea water temperatures is the cause of the extension in range of Atlantic Coast bluefish to the north and east. The north polar icecap has been receding for nearly two decades and, with some minor fluctuations, the trend in ocean temperatures has been upward. Basically, the species is taken from mid-Maine waters to Florida in the eastern United States. There is a considerable population of small fish in the southern part of the Gulf of Mexico that normally moves in summer into the upper part of the Gulf.

Although only a few specimens have been recorded off Bermuda, to the south in the Caribbean, particularly off Cuba, the species is common seasonally. Dr. Ruben Jaen of Caracas, in his book *Fishing in the Caribbean,* reported that bluefish (*anchoa*) abound around the island of Margarita, which lies off Punta Arenas in Venezuela, during February and March, then disappear for a time to return in July and August. This may well be due to spawning activity. Blues appear off the coast of Uruguay in April and May and, further north, off the coast of Brazil during June. As noted previously, this probably is another race which has adapted to warmer waters. Catches in commercial quantities are made off Argentina also, which seems to support this speculation.

Across the Atlantic, bluefish range from the Azores and the coast of Portugal southwards to, and around, the Cape of Good Hope in Africa. Migrations also pass through the Strait of Gibraltar and into the Mediterranean.

The Black Sea population is of different stock, with the fish moving seasonally between the Black Sea itself and the Sea of Marmara to the south. Ali G. Pasiner of Istanbul, Turkey, who is an eager bluefisherman, has informed me that Black Sea blues virtually disappeared in this area in one of the fish's unpredictable cycles of scarcity.

In the Pacific, bluefish are limited in range primarily to the eastern and western coasts of Australia, Tasmania, the Tasman Sea between Australia and New Zealand, and around New Zealand itself. In the eastern part of the Indian Ocean, throughout Indonesia and around the Malay Peninsula, confusion among native populations concerning names of particular fish has caused equal confusion as to presence of bluefish. Some reports are of doubtful origin while others have been made by trained fishery biologists. In any case, it is evident that blues are not plentiful in that large expanse of water and may be considered casual visitors. On the western side of the Indian Ocean, however, many catches have been recorded in the Madagascar area. Presumably these fish are part of the South African stock.

SCHOOLING

No matter where they may be found, blues swim in much the same manner throughout the world. They keep swimming from the time of birth until death. They cannot rest stationary in the water column, as can many other species, since forward motion is required to keep water moving over their gills. Snappers will stick together in rather tightly packed schools so that, if you find one snapper, you will find many others. As each individual fish grows, it tends to space itself more widely from its companions, so the schools cover a wider area. When they approach the ten pound mark, the number of individuals in a school drops. Often these larger specimens will be in groups of only a half dozen, or even may be loners.

In my own fishing, I have never noted that particular schools of blues are made up of one sex only. However, Al McClane, author and one of this country's top anglers, does a good deal of fishing in the Palm Beach section of Florida and has reported the contrary to me. One winter day, he caught four big blues to a top of about 12 pounds and all were males. On subsequent trips, even larger specimens were taken and all were of the same sex. This may indicate that larger blues separate by sexes at certain times in their life cycle.

Separation of maimed or injured fish is well known off the coast of Hatteras, North Carolina. Every year both commercial and sport fishermen take scarred individuals from schools that arrive about two weeks ahead of the major migrations. The lame, the halt and the partially blind stick together with some sort of fishy understanding that they will not chew on one another. In the wild, these cripples would be destroyed by their healthy companions.

Bori L. Olla, who watched bluefish held in a huge tank at the Sandy Hook Marine Laboratory on a night-and-day basis, has told me some fascinating tales about their schooling behavior. There is a definite pecking order among individuals in a school, and one ends up as leader. If a new fish is introduced to the group, battles may result until the leader establishes its position as boss. When one blue lags behind the school regularly, the leader often will make a quick circle to the rear and nip the tail of the laggard.

At one point during this fish-watching experiment, Bori saw an unfortunate bluefish whack its nose against the glass of the aquarium and it was stunned momentarily. As it sank slowly, it was torn to pieces in a matter of seconds by its alleged friends. Even in the wild, such cannibalism is not unusual. On several occasions, I have found entire caudal fins lopped from a bluefish in the belly of one of its companions I have caught. Whether such attacks are made intentionally, or unintentionally when in a feeding frenzy, no one knows. At any rate, there is no question that big blues will gobble down smaller ones without any feeling for family and friends. In the Azores, a snapper is a common bait when fishing for jumbo blues. There is little wonder that the Hatteras "hospital" schools stick together!

FEEDING

No account of bluefish would be complete without citing the writings of Professor Spencer F. Baird made in 1874 in the report of the United States Commission on Fish and Fisheries. Authors have used the quotation below—with and without credit to the original author—have paraphrased it and have lifted sentences from it freely. I feel it can stand on its own merits.

> There is no parallel in the point of destructiveness to the bluefish among the marine species on our coast, whatever may be the case among some of the carnivorous fish of the South American waters. The blue-

fish has been likened to an animated chopping machine, the business of which is to cut to pieces and otherwise destroy as many fish as possible in a given space of time. All writers are unanimous in regard to the destructiveness of bluefish. Going in large schools, in pursuit of fish not much inferior to themselves in size, they move along like a pack of hungry wolves, destroying everything before them. Their trail is marked by fragments of fish and by the stain of blood in the sea as, where the fish is too large to be swallowed entire, the hinder portion will be bitten off and the anterior part allowed to float away or sink. It is even maintained with great earnestness that such is the gluttony of the fish that, when the stomach becomes full, the contents are disgorged and then again filled.

Professor Baird evidently did not believe the last sentence, and neither do I. The idea may have been generated by the fact that blues often regurgitate their latest meal when hooked or netted just before they are beached or boated. Many other species do the same.

Bluefish teeth, designed for gobbling anything smaller than the fish itself and also for inflicting wounds on careless anglers. Photo by Frank Woolner.

There is no question that bluefish will eat just about anything found in the areas in which they swim provided that an edible piece of the creature can be bitten off. A total of 83 different species have been recorded in bluefish stomachs by just one team of researchers. Even bottom feeding species are not safe from attack. In a July–August, 1972, issue of *Marine Fisheries Review,* an account of blues chomping happily on yellowtail flounder and sea robins, accompanied by some unusual photos of flatfish that survived even with large chunks missing from their anatomy, is detailed by Fred E. Lux and John V. Mahoney. At the time of the Civil War, there were many reports of bluefish driving every swimming creature from the waters of Boston Harbor.

Bluefish at times will even attack birds swimming on the surface, flying low and dabbling their feet, or even when diving in search of food. Gulls and terns will not rest on the water over surfaced schools of blues and do not dive after bait fish when these predators are active. Petrels, which work further offshore than most gulls and terns, often are missing a foot and their habit of dapping along the wave troughs undoubtedly lures bluefish to take a bite. In March of 1976 near Salter Path, Carteret County, North Carolina, Wildlife Resource Commission personnel picked up more than 300 dead horned grebes at the tideline. Autopsies on several of the grebes revealed needle-like punctures of legs, lower abdominal regions and even shoulders—typical of wounds inflicted by blues. In brief, a hungry bluefish will tackle anything at hand until something more tasty swims along.

Despite many reports during World War II that giant bluefish attacked downed aviators and injured seamen off the North African coast, I can state flatly that this never happened. I personally traced down some of these rumors at the time and they were all just that—rumors. However, blues have severely bitten swimmers and waders occasionally, whether by design or by accident no one knows.

On April 10, 1973, during brisk winds, murky water and a heavy run of mullet inshore, anglers at Haulover Pier near

Miami had a field day at high tide catching blues up to 20 pounds. A year and two days later, there was a similar run and bathers in the surf were attacked ferociously by the fish. At least eleven people were treated for wounds and four went to the hospital. One young girl had to have 55 stitches taken in her leg. She reported that she saw the fish bite her, back off, then take another bite before she ran up onto the beach screaming. Since that date, lifeguards in the area now order all bathers out of the water when the combination of wind, murky water and mullet occurs. Similar attacks on swimmers have been reported elsewhere along the coasts with one spectacular blitz in 1985 during Easter weekend at Nags Head, North Carolina, when 13 people were treated for major wounds on feet and ankles. Again, there were masses of bait in rather murky water.

While being unhooked, blues will slash a human thumb, toe or other bit of anatomy when given the chance. This is the only species of true fish—not shark—I have found that will take definite aim at a presumed enemy even when out of water. I have scars to prove it.

At times, bluefish can become highly selective in their feeding habits. A clue to one reason for such selectivity was given in the June, 1970, issue of *Copeia,* a scientific journal which cannot be considered standard bedtime reading for anglers. Bori L. Olla, Harvey M. Katz, and Anne L. Studholme, researchers and fish watchers at the Sandy Hook Marine Laboratory, wrote an article based on observations made at the Laboratory tank.

Without going into all the details, let me outline the findings. Blues were swimming in a school in the tank. Food, in the form of live mummichogs (known also as killifish), was tossed into the tank. The individual baits were small. When they hit the water, the bluefish broke out of their schooling formation and started to swim more rapidly.

When an individual bluefish sighted a mummichog, its eyes would turn forward and it would head full steam towards the victim. If it missed, it would turn, slow down, and start searching for another mummichog. Lesson number one for the angler: if a blue misses your lure, present it again in the same area just as soon as possible.

When the blue did not miss, it opened its jaws, arched its head, and gobbled the minnow down. Immediately, it would turn 90 to 180 degrees from the direction of attack; then, after swallowing its prey, would move back into the area where the food was first found. Again, this indicates that a fisherman should cast or troll over the same water even after a fish has been caught. There may be others which were beaten to the target.

After the bluefish had been satiated with a full meal of small mummichogs, they tended to stop searching for more food in the same area and returned in general to a schooling formation at slower swimming speed. However, when a bait of larger size was then introduced into the tank, the blues went back to the attack—evidently polishing off the meal with a heavy dessert. The obvious lesson for the angler is: when strikes fall off among a feeding school of blues, switch to a larger lure or natural bait. According to the researchers, chances of success are increased by as much as 90 percent—if fish in the open ocean behave as they did in the tank. It seems highly probable that they would behave in the same manner, for the specimens in the Sandy Hook aquarium were not exposed to the sight of their keepers.

Food supply of course influences local movements of bluefish in any coastal area once the main migrations have arrived. They will not stay in a section that is a biological desert and tend to congregate where bait is readily available. I will go into this in more detail when discussing the best waters for fishing. Just how much effect the food supply has on the migrations themselves is unknown.

Water temperature, however, has a major effect on these migrations and also on the activity of the fish themselves. In captivity, the lower limit of tolerance among bluefish appears to be about 52 degrees Fahrenheit. In the wild, they apparently can stand water almost ten degrees colder. When the thermometer reaches 85, blues show signs of extreme distress and try to move elsewhere. Their ideal aquatic climate appears to be about 68 degrees. Obviously, therefore, if a cold current below 60 hangs off a portion of the coast, bluefish will avoid it in favor of something more to their liking. Such thermal barriers are fairly common, particularly during the early part of the season. For example, in 1972 anglers at Montauk, New York, noted a scarcity of blues in inshore waters even though fish were plentiful in areas to the east and west. Aerial temperature observations revealed that a wedge of cold water hung in an eddy off the eastern end of Long Island most of that summer and blues evidently ran offshore around it.

In studying geographical ranges through which fish travel and accompanying water temperatures—the classic approach to research on marine species—temperatures played an important part in the Sandy Hook program. However, something else also appeared to be involved. It might well be light, which is known to influence migrations of many types of fauna.

At the Sandy Hook tank Bori Olla and Anne Studholme discovered several points. First, bluefish tend to school together and swim more rapidly during daylight hours than during darkness, hence are more active when the sun is up. Also activity was increased at a more rapid rate "from the last hourly reading before light onset to the first reading after light onset." In brief, go fishing just before daylight and fish until sunrise. I and thousands of others have found this an excellent rule while bluefishing. In the laboratory, the fish's swimming speed slowed as darkness approached, so the hours just before and just after sunset, normally good for anglers, seem to break rules.

Finally, it appeared that bluefish have a built-in time clock of some sort so that they can determine the hours of dawn and dusk even when the light stimulus is removed. Again, anglers will agree, for fish in the wild will hit best during those hours even when the sky is covered with heavy clouds. This time clock evidently operates to some degree also with respect to seasonal migrations.

All natural conditions cannot be duplicated in a laboratory tank. At times, bluefish in the ocean will feed ravenously in the dead of night. When I first became an avid surf fisherman for blues after the end of World War II, it was common knowledge that fishing at Great Point, Nantucket, came to a halt when it became totally dark. This is no longer true either at Nantucket or elsewhere along the coast. Party boats operating off New Jersey now specialize in night fishing. Surfmen have good success almost everywhere after sundown. Whether the fish have changed their habits or whether the increased number of anglers willing to give up sleep is the cause is anyone's guess. Note, however, that when artificial lures are used during darkness, they should be fished far more slowly than during daylight hours.

MIGRATION AND CYCLICAL PHENOMENA

If the complicated migratory game of musical chairs along the Atlantic seaboard is only vaguely understood, it still can be classified as crystal clear when compared to the causes of wild fluctuations in the abundance of bluefish in the same area over a period of years. These cycles of plenty and scarcity were first described by Zacceus Macy in his *Account of Nantucket* as follows: "From the first coming of the English to Nantucket (1659), a large fal-fish, called the blue-fish, thirty of which would fill a barrel, was caught in great plenty around the Island from the 1st of the sixth month till the middle of the ninth month. But it is remarkable that in the year 1764 . . . . they had all disappeared and that none have ever been taken since. This has been a great loss to us."

Tracing the rise and decline of cycles as far as bluefish are concerned is difficult because these cycles varied widely on different sections of the coast. Indeed there is good argument that the word "cycle" should not be used at all since it means something very periodic—and there has never been anything very periodic about the rise and fall in abundance of blues. When there is a glut of fish off the Virginia Capes, for example, they may well be scarce in Massachusetts.

Variations in water temperature may be a contributing factor, but cannot explain fully the fluctuations in the bluefish supply. Blame has also been attached to the lack of bait as can be illustrated by the following quotation from a fascinating article published in the January 6, 1883, weekly edition of *The American Angler*. The author, who called himself Old Isaak, was on board the sloop *Katy* sailing from New York City to Fire Island. "The water was perfectly alive with fish (be it remembered this was twelve years ago)," he wrote. "The fish-oil factories had not cleaned out the menhaden (mossbunkers), the food fish *par excellence* of all salt water game fish. I repeatedly killed bluefish and mossbunkers on the surface with my revolver. Yet the high, but comparatively smooth sea, made me often send lead in vain. With a shotgun, I could have killed hundreds of mossbunkers in an hour."

Old Isaak's trip, it should be noted, was liberally laced with dippings from jugs of whiskey and rum, and apparently all of his companions were armed to the teeth. Such a venture I am always glad to avoid!

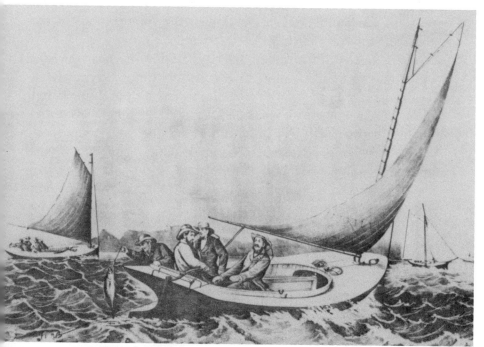

Trolling for bluefish with metal lures before the days of the internal combustion engine.

In addition to temperature fluctuations and bait supplies, the abundance of other marine species—or lack of them—has also been linked with bluefish supplies. Some claim that, when weakfish are scarce, blues are plentiful and *vice versa*. In examining records, this has been true in some years, completely untrue in others. For example, in 1985 and 1986, both species appeared to be at a high peak from Cape Cod to the Carolinas. The every-so-many-years theorists in times gone by claimed that every seven, twelve, fourteen—or you name it—number of years bluefish vanished along the coast. Records again explode this type of statement. In brief, trying to explain the ups and downs with data available at the present time seems to be impossible.

Around 1810, blues were abundant south of Cape Cod, moved north of the Cape by 1837 and, in the 1850's, were everywhere even as far north as the Maine coast. The peak of this glut appears to have been reached in 1863 or 1864. By 1889, the fish had declined in numbers. Fish continued to be taken north of Cape Cod until 1910, even though the supply south of the Cape diminished radically.

There were various minor fluctuations for the next decade, but fishing was at a comparatively low ebb until 1927. After a slight increase in the early 1930s, the fishery all but disappeared until 1947, when snappers appeared in great numbers. By 1951, bluefish had reached glut proportions, although individual specimens rarely topped the seven-pound mark. With minor dips and peaks in the supply, there appears to have been a fairly steady increase all through the 1960s, and the fish were growing larger and larger.

By 1969, an angler taking a 15-pounder—a catch that would have made headlines in the 1950s—had done nothing unusual. Size of individual specimens and their numbers increased throughout the 1970s. No particular year classes of fish seemed to predominate from that time right up to the present. Snappers to jumbos showed up throughout most of their range with the latter, oddly enough, being plentiful at northern extremes in Maine and southern, in Florida. A sort of levelling off in overall supply during the 1985 and 1986 seasons still did not curtail coastwide catches to any great degree. With blues of all sizes present, collapse of the fishery appears unlikely—a statement that I may regret since such collapses are not unknown in bluefish history.

Although exact figures are almost impossible to obtain, recent estimates indicate that recreational fishermen catch approximately 33 million blues a year along the east coast from Maine through Florida. In a typical year, commercial catches average between five and ten percent of this figure. Because bluefish flesh spoils quickly, commercial demand has been limited. However, development of freeze-drying methods and possible expansion of foreign markets may boost the commercial take in years to come. Until that time, the species remains primarily a sport fishing target.

Catches of freak bluefish, characterized by physical deformities, reach a peak when there is a glut. Pug-nosed specimens, with the upper jaw apparently missing; those with duplicate or deformed fins, and other unusually marked and shaped individuals cause amazement in the angling world. In a normal year, presumably the few freaks produced in the spawning areas do not survive, or survive in such small numbers that they are not

A deformed bluefish with a triple caudal fin taken off the Florida coast.
Photo by Frank Woolner.

taken by fishermen. When the base population increases markedly, the number of freaks does also.

Cycles of abundance and scarcity may also be influenced to some degree by parasites in, and on, bluefish. Like most marine species, blues are subject to attack or infestation by all sorts of creeping, burrowing creatures which can, in some cases, kill their hosts. Obviously when the number of hosts increases, such parasites do also. It should be noted that the majority of such pests are found inside the body cavity of bluefish and therefore do not taint the flesh as far as human consumption is concerned. Even the few that actually burrow into the muscle wall are rendered harmless by proper cooking.

A prime example of a parasite that needs a great many bluefish in its vicinity to maintain its life cycle is *Linoneca ovalis,* termed by scientists a "protandrous hermaphroditic isopod." The critter starts life as a male and attaches itself to the fish's gills, where it feeds off blood. It then develops further and moves into the mouth of the fish. There it simply sits, turns into a female and does not feed. The female form is then fertilized by a male from the gills and raises 60 to 120 larvae in a brood pouch. After developing, the larvae leave the host fish for the open ocean and swim about looking for another host. Unless bluefish are schooling close together, the larvae die since they cannot survive long without a blood meal. This parasite is normally found in blues weighing three pounds or less, probably because the larger fish are not packed together closely enough for the larvae to survive the ocean journey from one blue to another.

Another more lethal parasite is a long, purple, worm-like critter with a name unknown to me. In the 1960's, it infested the roe sacs of female blues throughout much of the northeast coast. This worm apparently rendered the eggs of the fish useless, for the roe that had been attacked hardened into a stiff mass. A similar infestation throughout the whole bluefish world naturally would result in spawning failure. Spawning success of course is the basic reason for the fluctuations in supply. Since no one knows just what requirements are needed to produce a dominant year class that will keep the fishery going over a period of years, speculation in this area is futile.

My own particular theory to explain the abundance of bluefish for more than a decade, or to explain it in part, is neither patented nor even perhaps, realistic. However, I submit that fishing effort, both sport and commercial, has increased substantially in recent years. This means that more fish have been removed from the ocean so that the total population has been kept at a fairly stable level. As a result, the tremendous gluts of the past have never been realized. Nature's balancing act among food supplies, parasites and diseases has been stabilized to some degree. Blues are among the few fishes which literally can eat their road to destruction by depleting their own food supply.

Perhaps another contributing factor in maintaining fairly stable population levels is predation. Small blues are eaten by a wide variety of marine species, including adults of their own kind. Few predators, however, will tackle a fully grown adult. The mako shark is the exception. The National Marine Fisheries Service has estimated that makos contribute to bluefish destructions to the tune of between five and 17 thousand tons a year. The population of makos in the Atlantic has been increasing slowly and even the lower five-thousand-ton figure must have some effect on the total bluefish supply. Bluefin tuna also will feed heavily on blues at times and are often used as tuna bait by anglers fishing in New England waters.

As far as the future is concerned, prospects are bright that supplies of blues will continue for some years to come at a high level. More and more interest is being expressed in factors influencing cycles of plenty and scarcity, economic value of the fishery when sport fishing is compared to commercial fishing, and in possible management measures. As this is being written, the Atlantic States Marine Fisheries Commission is mounting a three-pronged attack on bluefish problems: to analyze the data base concerning catch statistics, to assess the stocks available, and to weigh the economic value of the fishery with regard to all users.

One final gem of information before discussing the waters in which bluefish are found: the species is left-eyed. This means that, all other factors being equal, a bluefish will approach its potential meal normally with its left eye focussed on it first. If an angler has a choice, he should present his lure to that same eye if possible.

When I mentioned this rather unusual fact to Bernard "Lefty" Kreh, marine fly fisherman extraordinary, he was not at all surprised. Evidently Florida charter boat skippers have found that billfishes also are left-eyed. Lefty, who is left-handed but right-eyed, reported that a bait presented to the left side of a sighted billfish was taken more readily than one presented to the right eye of that same fish.

Left-eyed, right-eyed, or ambi-optic, it makes little difference to me. I plan to keep fishing for blues until they are no longer with us or until I am unable to hold a rod. It seems probable that the latter condition will pertain long before the former.

2

The Waters

Its crest curling in a hiss of foam, a wave rolls towards the shore, breaks with a muffled rumble, then sucks back seaward in the trough, carrying countless particles of sand with it as it retreats. Tiny mole crabs, sand fleas and a host of other creatures living at the ocean's edge burrow frantically to maintain a fragile hold on their shifting home site. If swept to sea, death in the form of a hunting predator awaits, and a small predator in turn may be gobbled down by a larger one at any moment. Add to this miniature scene of marine carnage flocks of seagulls and terns, scampering shorebirds dipping their bills in the wash with the speed of sewing machine needles, and there is good reason to understand why the life expectancy of minuscule ocean organisms is short.

Basic in the food chain of the sea is plankton—micro-organisms of all sorts, which include algae, eggs of sea creatures, bits of plant life both dead and alive, and a host of diatoms. These last form the link between plants and animals in the ocean environment. Their own life span often may be measured in hours. When they die, their minute skeletons form kieselguhr, which contributes to the layers of sediment on the ocean floor. (I include this bit of information for the benefit of those who, like myself, are fascinated by words and tend to collect bits of trivia with which to startle their friends.)

SNIFFING OUT FISH

Flowering diatoms—those that are in the process of reproducing their kind—help the bluefisherman. They are the cause of the bluefish "smell," a distinctive odor which may be sniffed at the range of a mile or more when the wind is right. Newcomers to the ocean scene often wrongly scoff at the old-time sniffer. When trying to find good water, you should never neglect your sense of smell.

Years ago, James R. Bartholomew, scientist, poet and fisherman, then connected with the old Farlow Herbarium at Harvard University, described this luscious scent in *Salt Water Sportsman* magazine. "Plankton, like Chanel Number 5, has a bouquet all its very own," he wrote. "It is like a cross between a pea soup fog on the Grand Banks and a crate of honeydew melons. It is fishy, but not too fishy. It is clean, fresh, with a hint of musky sweetness that no fish ever has until it is sizzling in the fry-pan with pork scraps and a touch of Madeira."

I cannot improve upon this description. However, I now question seriously whether this particular plankton bloom attracts small bait and therefore attracts blues to the area. I have a feeling that the fish themselves produce the plankton, oil or whatever it may be. Many others agree with my supposition.

Let me cite an example. While driving down the outer beach of Great Point on Nantucket, which is a prime bluefishing area, the late Francis W. Davis and I were keeping a sharp lookout for working terns or other indications of activity. Suddenly, fifty yards offshore, an oily slick bubbled to the surface, spread rapidly, and the air was filled with the fragrance of cucumbers, melons, Madeira and what-have-you. Bluefish, without question.

Jumping out of the car and grabbing our surf rods from the roof rack, we aimed two metal jigs in the direction of the slick and within seconds were each fast to a blue. Now that slick, with its characteristic odor, had come to the surface in the short time required to spot it while we were driving the beach. I submit that, if the plankton bloom took place at that moment, bluefish would not have had the speed necessary to vector in on the area within so few minutes.

In addition, if flowering diatoms with this particular scent attract bait, which in turn attract blues, why are not other species equally attracted? Striped bass, weakfish, bonito, channel bass and many other species are often found in the same waters. It seems logical that they would gather around the same slicks, but normally do not do so until long after the skim on the surface has been widely dissipated. Note also that several of the species give off characteristic odors of their own, with or without slicks. Years ago, Frank Woolner—editor, author and expert angler— theorized that every species may leave a scent trail of sorts, just as a bounding cottontail leaves a trail for a beagle on land. Recent research, particularly on various species of tunas, has proved that this is indeed the case.

I have even gone so far as to scoop up some of the floating scum—for want of a better word—and have examined it under magnification. Plankton certainly is visible in considerable quantity, yet there appears to be an oily substance mingled with the various diatoms. I am no chemist and am unable to analyze the material, but some angling laboratory man might make himself famous if he did so. Who knows? The substance might be produced artificially to become the finest bluefish attractor known.

Before leaving the subject of bluefish slicks, note that it is best to cast to or troll along one edge of the oily area rather than to play the middle. You may well take a fish if you hit dead center, but your chances of taking a second are greatly reduced, for the hooked blue's activity tends to cause the line to hit others and the school may well be spooked.

SIGHTING FOR FISH

Visual indications of bluefish are many. Obviously good fishing water is where the quarry may be seen slashing bait. Oddly enough, many anglers do not identify what they are seeing. Time after time, I have watched boatmen speed at full throttle in the direction of breaking fish only to discover upon arrival that they are not bluefish at all.

There are many species of both bait and sport fishes which feed at, or near, the surface. The eruption of a bluefish school, however, is distinctive. Blues appear to hit bait from all angles and over a fairly wide area. Most important, they all attack almost simultaneously so that the water appears to explode. However, when not feeding, blues sometimes travel at the surface with their dorsal fins occasionally breaking water. Cast a plug ahead of the moving school and chances of a strike are good. Cast right into the school and, nine times out of ten, all the fish will vanish quickly into the depths.

Menhaden and mackerel will ripple the surface in much the same manner as cruising blues. However, the former are readily identified by the bronze color of their backs and the latter are far more tightly grouped than bluefish. Weakfish and striped bass cause commotion on the surface when they are feeding, but the water does not turn white for a moment to calm down sometimes only a few seconds later. These two species attack bait more as single individuals rather than as a slashing school. Pollock are more sedate and slow-moving than blues when harrying feed on the surface. The same is true of members on the jack family in southern climes. Bonito come close to duplicating the flurry made by bluefish when seen at a distance, yet, at close range, they are easily distinguished from the toothed killers by body outline and color.

No matter how much I might write on this subject, it would be impossible to describe the exact appearance of a school of blues feeding on the surface. The knack of making quick identification comes only through long experience. Even the experienced, including myself, are fooled at times.

As mentioned earlier, during the late 1940s and throughout the 1950s bluefish were expected to stop hitting after dark. They have since changed their habits. Similarly, surfaced blues turning the water white in a feeding frenzy were the rule rather than the exception during that same period. Today, for reasons unknown, in many areas such activity is rare. As a result, fishermen depending upon sighting of schools are under a handicap and can only hope that the fish will return to their old ways of surface feeding.

If you can cover the water through which a school has passed, it is easy to determine their identity. Bits of bait, injured and maimed bait fish, and blood will be much in evidence. Chances are good that the blues will not be far away.

The practice of chasing bluefish schools along a beach or with a boat can be one of the most frustrating experiences in angling. The cusses will surface for a short time, then sound at the crucial moment, only to appear again in a minute many yards away. In such circumstances, unless there is a particularly strong current carrying bait and blues along rapidly, I strongly recommend that you stay where you are. The feeding fish often will return within a reasonable period.

The strong current exception is best illustrated by an example. The late Dr. Malcolm K. Johnston was among the first in modern times to develop surf fishing for blues to a fine art. He often told me of sighting a school off the beach at Monomoy Point, which forms the southern spur of Cape Cod. As the fish approached with a brisk current running parallel to the shore, he cast, hooked up, fought and landed a fine specimen. Bait had been carried down current about 50 yards during this procedure, so he sprinted in the soft sand, cast again to the edge of the school, and again hooked another of his quarry. This process was repeated five times, at which point Doc collapsed, exhausted, on the sand. I chuckled when he first told this tale. Two years later in exactly the same place, the same thing happened to me! Five casts, five sprints and five fish was my physical limit also.

If the current is swift and the school obviously is moving with it, it pays to chase the wanderers by beach or boat. However, work the edges of any such schools and, if afloat, do not drive through the center. There is a special place across the River Styx made for boatmen who speed full throttle through the middle of surfaced bluefish. After my Navy days, I drew up blueprints for a small, but efficient, torpedo which could be launched by hand to speed such knuckleheads to their just reward. I never got it into production and sometimes regret my failure to do so.

One of the best visual signals to assist in the spotting of blues is bird action. During migration peaks of bluefish, I have seen gulls and terns working over stretches of water that covered miles. Frantic bait trying to escape the toothed predators under the surface fall easy prey to their aerial attackers.

Any feeding seabirds are worth investigating, but if blues are your target, watch actions of the birds carefully. If they dive under the water to pick up bait, it is almost a certainty that the fish driving the bait are not bluefish. The fish will attack a submerged bird. Three times in my bluefishing life I have seen young terns disappear after having dived into a school of feeding blues. Once, I saw a full grown herring gull, crippled so that it could not fly, torn to pieces by the fish. They are not gentle!

Following feeding birds is a common practice among boat anglers. In crowded waters, it can become a nuisance, for the entire fleet will head towards the commotion. Captain Frank T. Moss, retired charter boat skipper formerly based at Montauk, New York, had a well deserved reputation among anglers as a bluefish guide. As a result, his every maneuver often was followed by many other boatmen when he attempted to zero in on feeding terns and gulls.

To lure the crowd elsewhere, Frank would slyly drop a good supply of crumbled bread or crackers over the side. The birds screamed and dove for the free meal, the fleet moved in, and the skipper quietly sailed away to an area where competition was not so keen while other craft circled the marine bakery in vain.

In clear water, blues often may be spotted even when they are not breaking water. Polarized glasses are extremely helpful in reducing surface glare for such spotting. Learn to look through the water rather than at it. A good way to master this technique is to wade out waist deep and then examine your toes, booted or otherwise. You will soon be able to ignore the surface light and distinguish submerged forms. Peering into the curl of a breaker is second nature to a surf fisherman. When dark, moving shadows are distinguished, the action starts.

In a feeding frenzy, blues at times will drive bait right onto the beach. Mangled and flopping small fish at the ocean's edge are a sure visual sign that bluefish are present. In the early winter of 1972, along the Outer Banks of North Carolina, locals took advantage of just such a phenomenon. Many of them dropped rods and reels, picked up gaffs, and waded into the blitz waters to take fish in quantity. This may hardly be sporting, yet perhaps is justifiable when a broiled filet is at a premium. Some even grabbed the frenzied choppers with their bare hands, a practice I do not recommend.

Height is a distinct advantage when trying to spot any fish underwater. The flying bridge or tuna tower on a boat gives the angler a much better picture of what goes on under the surface. Years ago some surf fishermen even lashed light aluminum ladders onto the rear of their beach buggies, then climbed them to get a gull's eye view of what went on in the wash. Birds use altitude when searching for prey: anglers should do the same even when not airborne.

If you are fortunate enough to have a light plane at your disposal, bluefish may be distinguished rather easily from other schooling species. Do *not* look for a fish colored blue. Look instead for liquid shadows, normally darker than the ocean floor, which blend with the water surrounding them whether that water be blue, green, or a murky gray. Striped bass from the air have a brownish cast to their backs; channel bass are coppery; bonito and jacks are of a different shape than blues, as are most other semi-tropical species; weakfish are silvery. George Bonbright, who was a pioneer fly fisherman in marine waters in the early 1900s, described bluefish as lying like huge, shadowy lead pencils when they could be seen through the surface glare. This is as good a description as any, and the color of the pencil adapts to the bottom over which it lies.

Color of the water itself is another visual indicator of where blues may, or may not, be. As a general rule, they do not like swimming in a muddy environment. The water need not necessarily be crystal clear, for much of the littoral ocean that is cloudy is rich in plankton, yet quantities of silt or sand in suspension will cause bluefish to move elsewhere. If bait is particularly plentiful, however, the fish will often invade murky waters which they would normally shun.

Oddly, suspended material in the water seems to bother large fish more than it does snappers. With their smaller gills, the youngsters would be expected to avoid granules that might irritate membranes or even suffocate them, but such is not the case. I have taken snappers from roiled water that would cause any self-respecting adult to swim far away.

Blooms of algae, such as the "red tide" first reported in the Bible when waters of the Nile turned to blood, will cause blues to avoid some coastal areas. Found at times along much of the Atlantic Coast, this micro-organism of the genus *Gonyaulax* can kill the fish if they fail to take evasive action. In 1985 and again in 1986 a new "brown tide," caused by a single cell plant identified as *Aureococcus anorexefferens,* turned waters of many Long Island, New York, bays the color of milk chocolate with the result that bluefish and swimmers went elsewhere. Unfortunately we can do nothing to prevent such algae blooms.

If a distinct line between two types of water not afflicted with algae can be seen, as is the case at the edge of the Gulf Stream or where a tidal river meets the sea, fish the clearer water. However, let the lure pass very close to the demarcation line, for plankton and bait are apt to be concentrated at that point. When afloat, the boat may well be in the murky section in order for the hooks to trail at the payoff edge.

SALINITY

Salinity should also be considered when seeking out good bluefishing waters. Rarely, if ever, will blues venture into purely fresh coastal rivers. They will chase bait schools into a tidal estuary that is brackish, but when all salt is missing, they turn tail even if the foraging is good. As is true in the case of murky water, the smaller specimens apparently can stand extremes better than their parents. Snappers therefore will be found farther up-current than adults. Anglers are not in the habit of carrying salinometers in their tackle boxes. A simple taste test will serve the purpose. If there is no salty tang on the tongue, look elsewhere for blues.

In years of drought and hot summers, which seems to have been the recent rule in the Chesapeake Bay area, salt water will move further up into a bay or tidal river mouth. Bluefish move in along with this saline intrusion and will be found well up-current or upstream of their normal feeding grounds. Often the invaders will drive all other species which favor brackish water out of the area.

CURRENTS

In the vast majority of cases, the bluefisherman will be faced with a wide expanse of ocean, no birds screaming and dipping, no fish in sight—in fact no indication that the sea is anything other than a biological desert. What then?

Look for a clash of currents. Such spots may be in many forms, such as tide rips, river water meeting the ocean, or turbulence over a reef or bar. They may extend for miles, as is true of The Race at the eastern end of Long Island Sound off the Connecticut shore, or may be only a few feet in diameter as in the case of a current eddy swirling behind a rock. Although bluefish may pass through water which is undisturbed by backwashes and swirls, usually they are transients only through such areas. Where the currents meet, they tend to lie for long periods, often many hours.

The reason for this is simple. Take a fish—any fish. Note that its back normally is of a much darker shade than its belly. If an individual fish is subjected to the same amount of light from above and below, on back and belly respectively, from its youth, scientists have shown that the demarcation line almost disappears. Coloration is practically the same throughout its entire body. Nature probably planned the dark back and light underside so that predators from above would have difficulty spotting their meal against the comparatively dark ocean floor or water depths, while predators from below would have similar trouble outlining their quarry against a lighter sky. Tip that same fish on its side or back and it becomes highly visible.

Visibility may be only momentary as a bait fish is tumbled, out of control, in a current, but a hungry bluefish lurking down-current needs only a moment to zero in on its target. Even such natural foods as squid, which do not have sharply contrasting colors on back and belly, can be seen more readily when flipped tentacles-over-eyes by an unexpected water force. Like a teenager falling downstairs, the bait becomes all arms and legs. Undoubtedly, also like a teenager, squid and other baits give off sounds of alarm under such circumstances, and the predator reacts.

Even in a flat calm, ocean waters are never still. The rotation of the earth sets up currents, effects of which are felt all over the world. Tides, produced basically by the gravitational pull of the moon and sun, add to this motion. The geographical configuration of both land masses and the ocean floor influence currents locally. Add winds, fresh water run-off from the polar icecaps and from rainfall over land, man-made structures in and over the water, and the equation becomes highly complex.

Nothing can beat local knowledge when it comes to determining the places and times of current clashes, where bluefish will be found. However, a stranger can prepare himself in advance so that his chances of success are improved. The first thing to remember is that the time of tide change is not necessarily the time of current change. For example, the flood tide current off Point Judith, Rhode Island, starts to move in a westerly direction approximately three hours before the actual time of low tide at that point.

Locals may memorize such specific bits of information, but those who wish to do some pioneering of their own should invest in the excellent *Tide Tables, East Coast of North and South America,* and *Tidal Current Tables, Atlantic Coast of North America.* These are published by the National Ocean Survey—a part of the National Oceanic and Atmospheric Administration under the United States Department of Commerce. They are available from a host of private agencies along the coast. Most major marine equipment dealers handle the publications. For local areas, daily newspapers regularly carry tide tables.

Equally important to a serious angler are nautical charts, published by the same agency and available at the same outlets. Water depths, configuration of the land, location of navigational aids, type of bottom, major tide rips, and many other factors important to successful bluefishing are indicated. Detail depends upon the scale of the charts purchased. The more detail, the better, so the few extra dollars invested in additional charts will pay off in fish caught.

Armed with charts, tide and current tables, an angler can do a good deal of homework prior to setting out in order to locate the best potential grounds. Equally important, he can determine in general the best times of day for fishing. Although on rare occasions I have taken blues when current or tide was slack, preferred conditions are when the water is moving swiftly. If a moderate wind is blowing against the flow of current, conditions may be considered ideal.

To generalize is dangerous, but I plan to do it anyway. In most areas, the two hours before and after the time of high tide, omitting the period of slack water, are usually most productive. As far as currents are concerned, the last hour of the current run in any given direction normally brings the best fishing.

There are obvious exceptions to these generalities. At the mouth of a tidal river or estuary, bait works into the shallows as the tide rises and flats are covered. Although small blues may follow the feed, larger specimens tend to wait until the tide starts to ebb and food is washed seaward. As the shallows are bared, minnows and the like are forced into the deeper channels and are carried by the current against their will to the open ocean. Lurking near the bars off the mouth, blues lie in wait to feast upon out-of-control small creatures. Under such conditions, the general rule concerning the last hour of the outgoing current holds, but that concerning high tide often does not. The first hour of the incoming current may be worthless due to lack of water depth, so this generality is also torpedoed.

Neophytes often have difficulty in believing that a current or tide change can make a tremendous difference when bluefishing. This was brought home to me while acting as "professor" at a special short course on marine sport fishing conducted annually under the sponsorship of North Carolina State University. The students, for the most part, were angling beginners of all ages. The group had embarked in various boats and all were trolling for small blues in the vicinity of Hatteras Inlet. Birds and fish were everywhere, excitement ran high, and I was spending a large proportion of my time untangling lines, advising all and sundry how to hook fish and not each other, and generally acting as a much-too-talkative mate.

Outlet of a typical tidal estuary is the ideal light tackle fishing water as the tide ebbs. Photo by Frank Woolner.

Within a matter of minutes, the tremendously fast fishing came to a screeching halt. Terns and gulls flew quietly to land and preened themselves while digesting their meals. The bluefish disappeared. Students looked around in dismay and obviously decided that some underwater calamity had taken place. In point of fact, the current had slacked and the fishing, as it turned out, was finished for the day. This made a good subject for my spontaneous lecture to the captive audience in the cockpit on the effect of currents on bluefish feeding habits, but I have a strong feeling that the students would have preferred more fish!

When currents are strong, areas where two currents move in opposing directions form turbulent disturbances easily seen on the surface. These are known as rips. Even when no winds blow, the water surface is rippled and remains so over a long period of time. Permanent rips are those which appear regularly, day after day, month after month, in approximately the same geographical position. Many, as noted above, are plotted on navigational charts.

Temporary rips are different. They may appear on one tide phase and vanish on another; be present when the wind blows from the northwest and disappear when it blows from the southeast. Configuration of the land and the ocean floor will influence these temporary rips considerably. Along sandy beaches these temporary rips may change their location after every major storm as the sand itself is shifted by water action.

The study of charts may be of some help, but study on the scene by means of a depth sounder is more practical in such cases. (Note in passing that such instruments used to be called fathometers as a generic term, but marine electronic equipment has become so sophisticated in recent years that the word has become an endangered species.) Where there is a sharp drop-off, chances are good that there will be a current clash of some sort at a particular change of tide. Note the location, fix the boat's position by loran, navigational aids or shore ranges, then mark the spot on your chart. Return to that spot when the currents change and you may well be successful.

The surf fisherman has no depth sounder at his disposal unless he is willing to go over the top of his waders, yet he can also spot such areas. My own procedure when fishing strange beaches is to visit the grounds at dead low tide. The offshore bars, sloughs—channels running parallel to the beach between it and an offshore bar—cuts in the bars, holes and underwater obstructions are revealed. By making a mental note of the best locations and, if necessary, by arranging driftwood or rocks to mark the key points, it is not difficult to return to payoff water when the tide is more favorable for fishing.

As is true in the case of tidal rivers and estuaries, bait fish will come into a slough through a cut in the offshore bar as the water rises. When the water falls again, bait will be washed to sea through the same cut. As a general rule, fish the inshore side of such cuts on the rising tide, the offshore side on the falling. Even when the bars are entirely covered, both bait and bluefish congregate at these points.

Although they can hardly be glorified by the name of rips, those spots on the down-current side of underwater obstructions often hold bluefish just as similar lies in fresh water hold trout. Again, bait is tumbled about as the current carried it by and the predator has easy pickings. Pinpoint casting from a small boat or from the beach soon separates the amateur from the experienced angler under such conditions.

This also holds true in the case of man-made obstructions as I found to my chagrin while pier fishing at Venice, Florida. The beach there is relatively unbroken in contour and the pier therefore is popular. One old timer, whose name I never learned, had staked out a claim on the down-current side of a particular piling. Almost toothless, he was sucking on an unlighted cigar, which grew smaller and smaller as time passed and as he derricked up bluefish after bluefish from a point almost under his feet. The blues were small, but they were a lot larger than the nothings I caught as I, and several others, danced around him in an attempt to reach the magic few feet of productive water.

Finally, I stopped fishing and engaged the ancient in conversation. My Yankee accent seemed to fascinate him and he con-

When anglers cannot reach good fishing water from the beach edge, a fishing pier is the answer. This is one of the longest on the Atlantic Coast at Myrtle Beach, South Carolina. Photo by Hal Lyman.

fided that he had fished that particular pier regularly ever since it had been built. After much observation and experimentation, he had discovered that many species, but bluefish in particular, hung around that individual piling at half tide. Obviously the bait supply and water conditions were ideal at that time.

While on the Florida scene, I should mention that adult bluefish in that state normally move into far more shallow water than they do along the northern Atlantic coast. Rips and inlets are still prime producers, yet the fish will be found in Florida areas that might be considered snapper waters to the north. The explanation for this behavior is simple: blues are slaves to their stomachs. On the long, sandy beaches, foraging is poor unless bait can be herded into the shallows. Inlets, piers and bridges of course produce the current clashes I keep emphasizing, but elsewhere the fish will feed on targets of opportunity and will even risk stranding as they pursue fleeing mullet.

SEA FLOOR AND WIND

Leaving currents and rips, let me look at the bottom of the sea for a moment. Fishermen often ask me whether or not bluefish prefer sandy, rocky, muddy, or shell bottom as their swimming grounds. There is no pat answer. I have caught them over the pure sands of Cape Hatteras beaches, the tumbled rock and clay off Gay Head on Martha's Vineyard, the "pluff mud" as the natives call the soft stuff in the channels of South Carolina's Cape Romain, and the oyster shells that pave parts of Chesapeake Bay. They feed where the food is found. If I were to say the type of bottom which blues seem to prefer when there is a choice, I would opt for something other than mud. If there is no choice, disregard this advice.

Wind, on the other hand, can have a major effect on bluefishing. In a flat calm, blues may feed and may be caught, but it is more difficult to persuade them to hit a lure or bait than when the ocean's surface is ruffled. Undoubtedly this is because they have a good look at the offering and can see that something is wrong with it. Active surf along a beach will bring blues in close, yet too much surf will roil the water and drive the quarry offshore. As previously noted, wind working against a current results in prime bluefishing conditions.

The direction of the wind also influences catches. What is a good wind for one area often is a bad one for another. For example, the dying away of a northerly storm often produces top bluefishing along the New England coast. Around Barnegat Bay, New Jersey, such conditions ruin the fishing and anglers pray for southerly breezes. For a visiting angler, the best bet is to inquire locally to determine just which wind direction is ideal.

Only one rule can be applied almost universally: over the long haul for the surf angler wind in his face will produce better reults than wind at his back. The reason for this is obvious—bait is driven close to the beach and the predatory bluefish follow it.

To describe every feature of good bluefishing water is almost impossible. A barren area may be transformed into an angler's heaven in a matter of moments if wind, tide, water and bait cooperate properly. If there is one general condition to avoid, I would classify dirty or extremely roiled water as this condition. There is even an exception here. When the sea is filled with a light, line-clogging algae known as goglum, blues seem to thrive in it. Water between the tiny weed patches is clear, but to move a line through the area is to dredge up pounds of the floating organisms. Lures that weigh a few ounces soon weigh pounds after a few feet of travel and their effectiveness is destroyed. Bluefish like goglum: I disagree with them.

There are times when all rules go by the board in waters where blues are known to be. I have seen it happen on many occasions from Cape Cod to the Florida Keys. Fishermen will be trolling and picking up one or two blues among an entire fleet. Frantic changing of lures produces little more. Often the scarcity of catches can be reversed by stopping the boat, shutting off the engine and casting a popping plug more or less at random in waters around the craft. Just why this can result in an eruption from the bottom of taking fish, I do not know, but the technique works well enough so that I recommend it on a regular basis. It is particularly effective when the seas are calm or with only a slight surface ripple.

PRIME WATERS

Over a period of more than 300 years, some bluefishing waters have stood the test of time. When the fish are on a down cycle of plenty, they will still be caught in reduced numbers on these grounds and, when the cycle swings upwards, they will return in numbers there before appearing elsewhere. In what follows, I have made no attempt to pinpoint exact locations, for this would be impossible due to shifting currents, bars and beaches. The general areas, however, will indicate where an angler has the best possible chance of taking adult bluefish. Note the qualifying "adult." Snapper grounds change so often that it is fruitless to mention them. A hot spot this year may be as cold as ice the next.

NOVA SCOTIA TO MASSACHUSETTS

With the warming of northern Atlantic waters in recent years, bluefish have been taken frequently in midsummer as far east and north as Saint Mary's Bay and the Annapolis Basin in Nova Scotia, but they must be considered targets of opportunity only, since there is no great concentration of fish. Off the coast of Maine, however, large blues now support a growing sport fishery. Strays are taken from waters around Mount Desert Island; however, best fishing is from the Muscongus Bay area westwards. The many tidal river estuaries in this area are prime grounds and the blues run well up into the bays until they hit water of low salinity. They are often found in company with striped bass.

As a quick aside, contrary to the belief of some, bluefish usually do not drive stripers away. Because they are quicker than the bass, they may beat the striper to a lure thus giving an angler the impression that there are no bass around. The two species may be found time and time again feeding together in a rip. Large bluefish may chomp on small stripers—and *vice versa*—in special circumstances, yet the two do not bother each other extensively when the food target is a third party.

Maine fishermen also find blues offshore on the tuna grounds, such as those off Boothbay Harbor. In addition, shoreline from Popham west through Old Orchard, Kennebunk, Ogunquit and York Beaches is favored surf fishing area. An interesting point concerning Maine's bluefish is that many of the tidal rivers host schools of very small snappers, evidently progeny from a special group of northern summer spawners. Just where the spawning grounds for this particular body of fish may be located is unknown.

New Hampshire's short coastline has never been renowned as a bluefishing area, but the glut in recent years has boosted its reputation to some extent. Inshore waters off both Portsmouth and Hampton have produced some good catches and party boat skippers, operating primarily during darkness, have done well. A few explorers have boated some large specimens off the Isle of Shoals with best fishing reported in early August.

Moving down the coast into Massachusetts, waters off the Merrimack River are frequented by blues normally from mid-July to September. Plum Island is a favored surf fishing area, but note that it is a wildlife refuge. This means that many sections of the beach are restricted during bird nesting season. From the rugged coastline around Cape Ann down to Nahant, bluefishing is primarily a summer affair with boat fishing predominating. For reasons best known to themselves, blues tend to feed deep throughout this area.

Although badly polluted, waters in Boston Harbor hold bluefish with best runs around mid-July and in September. If fishing for the table, waters east of Lovell's Island and as far out as the Graves are recommended to avoid the worst of the pollution. Small to medium blues work their way into Quincy, Hingham and Hull Bays and occasionally some much larger specimens are taken off the outer shore from Nantasket Beach. From Cohasset to Plymouth, fishing may be termed average, but then Cape Cod Bay is reached.

This section of the coast since Colonial times has been famed as excellent bluefish water. Throughout the Bay, thence around the tip of Cape Cod at Provincetown southward to the Cape's spur at Monomoy Point, fishing often starts prior to the first of June and runs well into October. From Monomoy to Great Point on Nantucket Island, there is a series of tide rips, highly dangerous in foul weather, which form one of the best bluefishing grounds in the Northeast.

Nantucket itself, with its neighboring small islands of Tuckernuck and Muskeget, has produced blues since the Indians were the only inhabitants. If there are any bluefish at all to be found in Massachusetts when the cycle is on the downswing, Nantucket is the place to find them. Nantucket Sound—bounded by Nantucket itself, Martha's Vineyard, and the southern shore of Cape Cod—is all good water. The fish arrive as early as mid-May and at that time normally are feeding at or near bottom.

From the Vineyard, which provides good fishing from both beach and boat, westward through Vineyard Sound, along the

Elizabeth Islands, and in Buzzards Bay, bluefishing can be considered a way of life. In years gone by, the season was considered over by the end of October, yet today anglers using deep jigging methods take blues well into November and might continue to do so if the New England weather was more kindly after Thanksgiving. It may be that bluefish winter over in those waters.

The connection between Cape Cod Bay and Buzzards Bay is one of many monuments to engineering knowledge found along the coasts. The Cape Cod Canal and other similar canals were all designed to permit passage of ships from one point to another without the risk of steaming through dangerous offshore waters. A side effect in such constructions has been man-made bluefishing grounds. Currents are swift, bait fish have a worrisome existence, and hungry blues take advantage of the fact. Do not neglect canals even when they are small in size. They have the advantage of being fishable when high winds make other coastal water untenable for the angler.

RHODE ISLAND TO NEW JERSEY

Moving down the coast, Nomans Land, mentioned earlier as a bluefish spawning area, is at the eastern border of Rhode Island Sound. Block Island is on the Sound's western edge. Both islands are surrounded by excellent fishing water, complete with rips, bars, beaches and rocky shallows. The water itself is exceptionally clear and on the average is considerably cooler than the ocean to the north and east. For this reason, blues normally arrive a bit later than they do off southern Cape Cod, yet the migrations in autumn will extend well into November.

Along the Rhode Island mainland, the various points are favored by both surf fishermen and boatmen. Watch Hill Point, Weekapaug Point, Point Judith, Brenton Point and the reef near it, Sakonnet Point and Beavertail Point are among the best known. On the Massachusetts islands, waters connecting tidal ponds with the sea are known as openings. In Rhode Island, they are called breachways. All of them, particularly on the outgoing tide, furnish excellent bluefishing. If you hear a Rhode Islander state that they are murdering them at Charlestown or Quonny Breachway, do not think that he is talking about a military action. Incidentally, when you look for Quonny on the chart, try Quonochontaug instead. Even American Indians shy away from its full title today.

In Colonial times, all of Narragansett Bay, even as far north as Providence where the water salinity drops, was good fishing water. With the arrival of the blessings of modern civilization, much of the area became so badly polluted that bluefish swam elsewhere. Fortunately, this trend has been reversed and, as the Bay became cleaner, bluefish returned. Although big choppers rarely appear in the upper reaches of the Bay, there is good bluefishing throughout the area. Because of private ownership and difficulties in reaching the shore overland, this section is best tackled via a small boat.

Block Island Sound is a sort of aquatic stopper at the entrance to Long Island Sound. Rips are plentiful, and so are bluefish. It is not water for a small outboard skiff, although many simpletons take their lives in their hands in such craft. All too often, they lose their grip.

Between Fishers Island and Little Gull Island lies The Race, which is the best known bluefishing area off the Connecticut shore. Here, depths exceed 200 feet and the water is seldom still. Blues congregate in the many rips and may be taken from the surface right down to the bottom. It pays to experiment by fishing at many levels until the payoff depth is hit. Again, a seaworthy boat is recommended, for seas may build up in very short order when currents turn against the wind.

Elsewhere along the Connecticut coast, best bluefishing lies from Sachem Head easterly to the Rhode Island border. The Falkner Island area south of Guilford; Six Mile Reef off Clinton; the Bloody Grounds, lying south of the Connecticut River mouth and northwest of Plum Island; the Gut, labelled Plum Gut on charts, between Plum Island and Orient Point on Long Island, and Harkness State Park near Waterford, are among the best known grounds. Until the population explosion of blues in recent years, waters west of Sachem Head produced little other than snappers. Today, larger specimens are now more common throughout much of the wide expanse included in western Long Island Sound waters, yet those that can classify as jumbos are rare indeed.

Although trolling and chumming were once the basic methods uséd by anglers in the Nutmeg State, more and more of them are turning to light tackle casting both from boats and from shore. Since the coast is dotted with islands, rocks and tidal streams of all sizes, it is ideal for this type of fishing. Each season turns up new fishing spots as fishermen of imagination continue to explore.

On the New York side of Long Island Sound, bluefish for reasons best known to themselves are not as plentiful as they are on the Connecticut side. The exception is the Montauk Point area, which technically delineates the limits of Block Island Sound rather than Long Island Sound. Shagwong Reef, Cerberus Shoal and the Cartwright Grounds south of Montauk are prime areas, yet the whole Montauk section, complete with tide rips both onshore and offshore, produces well from both beach and boat. The overwhelming number of charter, party and private boats attest to its popularity.

Perhaps more than anywhere else in the Northeast, Montauk catches are affected by water temperatures. Montaukers may complain about bluefish scarcity at times when fish are being slaughtered to the east, west and north of them. Almost without exception, the cause can be found with a thermometer. Eddies of cold water lying west of the Gulf Stream may persist for days and even weeks at a time off the Point, and these eddies act as an effective barrier to cruising blues.

The south, or ocean, shore of New York's Long Island has its best fishing at or near the main inlets: Rockaway; Jones, and Cholera Banks off that inlet; Fire Island; Moriches, and Shinnecock. This is logical, since concentrations of bait swept out of the bays are far greater than along open expanses of sandy beach. As is true in the Montauk area, the fish often will remain into late November unless a cold northeaster sends them scurrying to warmer climes.

Although water pollution and algae growth problems have hexed some bluefishing on the northern shore of Long Island, the species has been taken in recent years more commonly than since the early 1800s. The whole Gardiner's Bay area at the entrance to the Sound produces good catches. As an angler works westward, blues tend to decrease in size, but they are still available. Bluefish Shoal off Port Chester was not named for weakfish! The various points of land, such as Orient Point, Eaton's Neck and Lloyd Point, are more productive than flat beach areas.

Pollution is also a problem throughout the Hudson River Gorge, which runs something west of south out of New York Harbor to the edge of the Continental Shelf. Ocean dumping has been going on for many years in one section of the New York Bight and the bottom has become a biological desert. What few bluefish that are caught in the area are sorry specimens indeed with fin rot and other diseases evident. Action has been taken to move the dumping grounds out to sea, but it will take some time for the old grounds to return to normal and provide fishing.

Gluttony brings the blues to the less than pure waters that surge around Sandy Hook, New Jersey. The area teems with bait of all kinds and the choppers tolerate some pollution and move in. From the Hook to Cape May, Jersey has long been famed as a bluefishing area, and with good reason. South of Long Beach Island, the major runs are in the spring and fall with a few small specimens available all summer. North of that same island, there are many summer residents augmented at each end of the fishing season by migrants from other areas.

Up until the late 1970's, an incredible fleet of boats—party, charter and private—gathered off northern New Jersey and ladled out chum to such an extent that gourmets claimed the bluefish caught tasted of mossbunker. Today there is still an incredible fleet fishing around the clock, but chumming for the most part has given way to deep jigging and trolling. Whether or not the catches taste better is a matter of opinion!

The offshore fleet in northern Jersey is not the only taker of blues on that state's coast. Despite many claims from other areas, evidence is strong that surf casting with an artificial lure, using a rod and freespool reel, originated in New Jersey—and the basic quarry was bluefish. Casting a metal lure or "squid" gave rise to the term "squidding," which is applied today in many areas to all artificial-lure surf fishing.

I am not about to antagonize chambers of commerce along the Jersey coast by recommending one surf fishing or light tackle casting area over another. Suffice it to say that blues are found all along the shoreline during the seasons noted above. As elsewhere, the inlets—Shark River, Sea Girt, Manasquan, Barnegat, Beach Haven, Brigantine, Absecon, Great Egg Harbor, Corson and Townsend—provide prime angling. Access is sometimes a problem, but even among the crowded bikinis of Atlantic City fish may be taken. Small blues work up into the bays and sounds lying behind the barrier beach and, unless heavy rainfall brings too much fresh water runoff, light tackle buffs can do well.

For boat fishermen, the best known areas are in the general Sandy Hook section; Shrewsbury Rocks off Sea Bright; The Ridges off Manasquan, and waters off both Beach Haven and Barnegat Inlets. These are better known than similar waters to the south simply because the season runs from June through November—always providing that the weather behaves. Around Cape May, bluefish generally average smaller in size than those taken in more northern waters. Basically because nautical names fascinate me, I recommend giving Prissy Wicks Shoal a whirl, north of the Cape May Channel.

DELAWARE, VIRGINIA, AND THE CHESAPEAKE

Delaware's short Atlantic coastline from the Maryland border to Cape Henlopen has spring and fall fishing. This section is one of the very few where the spring run is heavier than the autumn one. The Hump off Indian River Inlet is the best known offshore spot. For the beach fisherman, Rehoboth and Bethany

Beaches are available, but, since the beaches themselves are un-broken, blues rarely stay in one spot for any length of time. Indian River Inlet is the best bet and small fish move into the channel south of Burton Island inside the inlet itself.

Pollution in Delaware Bay fortunately has been reduced sub-stantially in recent years and many species of fish have returned to those waters. Small boat operators take blues, most of them under five pounds, as far north as Bombay Hook. Due to low water salinity, Reedy Point may be considered the northern limit for bluefish except for snappers.

Roughly seven miles off the Atlantic coast of Maryland, there is an area which parallels approximately the coastal contour, from Fenwick Shoal through Isle of Wight Shoal south to Great Gull Bank, and that produces big bluefish from late May into July and again from about mid-September through November. Oddly, small blues hang around the two shoals mentioned even during the summer months. Maryland watermen have a descrip-tive name for small shoals—they call them lumps—and First Lump, west of Little Gull Bank, is a good trolling and chum-ming spot in spring and fall. Southwest and Southeast Lumps, roughly eight miles to the south, yield blues all summer long. The Jack Spot, famous for white marlin, also produces in spring and fall, much to the annoyance of skippers who have spent hours rigging baits for billfish only to have them torn to bits by bluefish.

Inshore, there is bluefishing along all of the Maryland Atlantic shore, with emphasis on the spring and fall runs for surf and small boat anglers. Small fish even work up into Isle of Wight Bay. I will come to the Chesapeake Bay side in a moment.

The northern end of Assateague Island is the best bet for surf fishermen who want bluefish. To the south and west, across the Virginia border, the island is channel bass water. Offshore, the Sugar Lumps and Winter Quarter Shoal are prime grounds and Blackfish Bank yields big fish in the late fall. As is true off Maryland, the many shoals that parallel the whole Virginia coast well offshore are good trolling and jigging grounds. To name them all would be to catalog the offshore waters.

Cape Charles and Cape Henry form the entrance to Chesapeake Bay. The spring run of blues in that area passes fairly quickly. From October even into January, weather permitting, the section from the Bay Bridge-Tunnel complex right into the open ocean produces spectacular fishing for what Virginians call jumbos. Mankind rarely improves salt water fishing by his construction efforts, but the Bay Bridge-Tunnel is a happy exception.

Moving north in Chesapeake Bay along both the Virginia and Maryland shores, the size of individual bluefish diminishes the further one gets from the ocean. The late William C. Schroeder, author of *Fishes of Chesapeake Bay,* reported that straggling bluefish appear in late March in Bay waters. Some may even winter over in the lower Chesapeake area during a mild winter. Although a few are taken around Swan Point Channel, in a normal season the Bay just north of the Annapolis Bridge may be considered their normal limit for all practical angling purposes. The exception: in years of drought when salt water intrudes well into the Bay, blues travel even further north.

With dozens of bait-filled rivers flowing into salt water, with hundreds of channels and inlets, with tidal conditions that may change at any time because of steady winds, with salinities varying greatly after a heavy rainfall, it is not extraordinary that bluefishing in Chesapeake Bay is not confined to a single spot. Among the better known areas are: Winter and Summer Gooses off the Choptank River mouth; the Hooper Island section; Northwest and Southwest Middle Grounds; the Windmill Point area, and Bluefish Rock off the mouth of the Back River. However, what is a good spot today may draw a blank tomorrow with a shift of wind. Local boat captains and news media outdoor reporters keep a close eye on movements of the schools and it is well to follow their advice.

Trolling has long been the favorite method of taking blues from Chesapeake Bay, but deep jigging and casting, particularly to surfaced schools, have become more and more popular. If angling from a boat, keep a close eye on the weather, for sudden squalls can change the Bay from a huge, serene millpond into a very dangerous stretch of water indeed. I learned this to my cost years ago when a small boat from which I was fishing south of Mobjack Bay swamped due to my own stupidity.

Returning to the ocean side once again, bluefish migrations cut in closer to shore from Cape Henry to the North Carolina line than they do in many areas. It pays to work along the beach and out to about five miles along Virginia Beach and the Sandbridge section. The waters four miles east of Sandbridge and the Tiger Wreck Lumps, another five miles east, are particular hot spots.

THE CAROLINAS, FLORIDA AND THE GULF

From the Virginia–North Carolina line to a point a scant two miles off Corolla, there is a similar stretch where big bluefish congregate during November and December. The Lumps, roughly 20 miles east of the state line, oddly enough plays host to many small blues on its western edge during July and August.

Fishing from surf and piers along Virginia Beach should not be neglected. Since the blues move in and out erratically, again advice of locals and news media people should be heeded. Similar fishing along the outer beaches of North Carolina is good for bluefish in spring and late fall when the larger fish sag inshore. Unfortunately, they do not do this on a regular schedule, but snappers and blues slightly larger can be taken almost throughout the year. As the Outer Banks area becomes more easily distinguished by its seaward barrier beaches—in general, the beaches from Duck Woods to Hatteras—fishing improves. Large fish in early spring and late fall, often into the winter months, appear from the tide line right out to the western edge of the Gulf Stream.

For boatmen, normally the best area for big choppers is about halfway between the shore and the Stream. Surf, pier, and small boat anglers must hope for bait close inshore; otherwise they must settle for smaller fish. However, these smaller specimens may be taken throughout most of the summer. They stick fairly close to shore and work up into the many sounds in the vicinity also.

Oregon Inlet, which separates Nags Head from Hatteras Island, is the first major break in the beach front working southward from the Virginia line. From the state line to the inlet, big blues are taken from both piers and the beach with November and December the best months. At Oregon Inlet itself, there is a major fishing center and marina with boats available to reach long-famous fishing grounds both inshore in the sounds and offshore to the edge of the Gulf Stream. This section of the coast down through Portsmouth Island forms the Cape Hatteras National Seashore, all prime bluefishing water.

Until James Hussey caught his record 31-pound, 12-ounce monster on January 30, 1972, most anglers felt that the New Year ended the bluefish season. Today, when weather permits, fish are found throughout most of the winter. Hatteras Inlet, between Hatteras and Ocracoke Islands, was the scene of Hussey's catch, but large fish sag in towards shore from time to time following vagaries of the Gulf Stream offshore and the bait supply carried by winds and currents from the sounds.

Waters off the entire Outer Banks area have been warmer than the long-term average in recent years. No one can state definitely that this trend will continue. It does, however, present a good argument in favor of the fact that blues move offshore to some extent during the winter rather than move south in a body. Given warm water, they simply stay where the feed is plentiful. If the water happens to be warm at the surf line, they will be there.

Miles of white sand beach extend along this shore of North Carolina. Surf fishermen look for breaks in the outer bars. Boatmen cruise around the dangerous waters between Diamond Shoals and the Gulf Stream. Small craft operators and waders cover the eastern part of Pamlico Sound. All of them take bluefish. Note that the big blues remain on the ocean side of the banks. Blitz fishing can happen along any part of the beach when weather conditions make angling possible. Because Cape Hatteras is the dividing point between temperate and semi-tropical waters on the eastern seaboard, temperature clashes between air and water often result in storms that make angling anything but possible!

The coastline cuts sharply westward south of the Cape and, although there is good bluefishing at times along the Ocracoke and Portsmouth Island beaches, chances are better for the fishermen who move well offshore to catch big fish. Core Banks and Cape Lookout National Seashore take over after leaving Portsmouth Island. This huge stretch of beach, extending to Cape Lookout itself, is lightly fished compared to the Nags Head–Hatteras area primarily because good harbors for offshore craft are not available until the Cape Lookout area is reached. For the surf fisherman, the various small inlets are the best bets. Cape Lookout Shoals produce the biggest blues for boatmen while shore-based anglers and small boat buffs take smaller specimens along Shackleford Banks to the north and west.

From Beaufort Inlet west along the Bogue Banks, thence southwest and south to Cape Fear and Frying Pan Shoals, the picture is similar. Small blues are taken from beach, boat and pier, particularly at the inlets—of which there are dozens—from April through November with normally a slack period during midsummer. Offshore craft based at Southport pick up some jumbo bluefish around Frying Pan Shoals and to the southeast of that area. Note that boatmen heading offshore along all of North Carolina's southwest coast undoubtedly would catch more large blues if they fished for them. Usually they are steaming to reach grounds where big game and the like are found. Also the season for taking migrating bluefish in those waters is earlier than that for offshore species in the spring, and later in the autumn.

West of Cape Fear thus to the South Carolina line, the picture is similar. Lockwood's Folly Inlet—I've often wondered what his folly might have been—Shallotte and Tubbs Inlets are the best areas. Fishing piers stud this part of the coast and many blues are taken off them from April right through November with a slump normal during the heat of midsummer.

A quick glance at a chart of the South Carolina coast shows immediately that its character is quite different from that of its neighbor to the northeast. Although there are some long expanses of sand, such as that at Myrtle Beach, there is no overall barrier stretching for miles with sounds lying behind it. The coast becomes more tropical in nature with hundreds of small islands, tidal rivers and streams. Flat tracts of marshland extend over acres of creeks and shallows. Nutrients in these marshes make this an important nursery ground for all sorts of game and bait fishes. Unfortunately these same characteristics do not make inshore waters the best for bluefish. Freshwater run-off tends to muddy the creeks and estuaries—and blues are not crazy about roiled water. Therefore look for South Carolina bluefish primarily seaward of the marshes.

From the North Carolina border to Murrell's Inlet, beach, pier and small boat fishing prevails and early spring is the best season. Scattered runs of blues weighing about three pounds last right into December off Myrtle Beach area piers with an occasional jumbo taken. Migrations of large fish normally pass well offshore. Working south and west, the area around North and South Islands is favored. The outer islands off Cape Romain, thence south to Charleston, furnish similar fishing.

Offshore, expanding fleets of charter and private boats in the resort areas around Charleston, Beaufort and Hilton Head head to sea primarily for other species. It is a long haul from that part of the coast to the Gulf Stream and anglers do not concentrate their efforts on blues. However, in recent years some jumbos have been taken during the late autumn months on live eels.

If you plan light tackle casting from any of the sod banks or marsh areas for small bluefish along the South Carolina coast, watch your footing carefully. I once vaulted neatly over the bow of a Boston Whaler near Cape Romain and sank almost instantly into "pluff mud" up to my waist. Extracting me from this gummy substance was a major effort on the part of my companions, and I thus learned the hard way to walk where running water could be seen and where the bottom was firm.

The southern coast of South Carolina and that of Georgia are very similar in character and in bluefishing possibilities. The series of islands, tidal streams and estuaries from Savannah to

Cumberland Island mean murky water inshore along most of Georgia's coast. Snappers and some slightly larger fish are taken from shore and pier as well as from small boats, but catches for the most part are incidental to those made when after other species. The Savannah area; Sapelo Island in McIntosh County; Sea, Saint Simons and Jekyll Islands near Brunswick, and Cumberland Island itself are the best known spots. As in South Carolina, this is because all are well known resorts. Best fishing is offshore where the effects of fresh water run-off are diminished. Late autumn and early winter produce the best runs.

The coastline bends westwards after crossing into Florida and, once again, its character changes with true barrier beaches separating bays from the Atlantic Ocean. The water is clear for the most part and blues are found all along the east coast. Seasonal runs of fish normally start in late September in northern Florida and are first taken from piers, beaches and small boats. As winter progresses, the fish move into the bays with small fish predominating. There is another less dependable run in the spring and a few comparatively small blues are taken all through the year after the majority swim northward. To list all areas where blues are caught would take a book in itself, but I will try to hit the hot spots.

From Fernandina Beach to Cape Kennedy, a few jumbo bluefish have been taken in recent years, but the average size is less than that of fish taken further north and south. Probably the main migrations of big fish are well offshore at the edge of the Gulf Stream. Their smaller brethren concentrate around the inlets. Action can be fast from piers and beaches when feeding blues chase bait right up to the shoreline. This same type of action is common at Cocoa and usually is sparked by a northeast blow.

A stretch from the Jensen Street bridge south for about five miles is a particularly hot area for shore casters. The Crossroads, a section at the junction of Indian River—actually a lagoon—and the Saint Lucie River, is an excellent fishing ground from October through March. Several spots there produce extraordinarily large bluefish equal in weight to those found almost anywhere along the coast. When the sun is high, such catches are rare, but at dawn, dusk and during night hours, results can be startling on these winter-overing fish.

The inlets at Salerno, Juno and Riviera Beaches are other sections where a northeast wind brings the blues close to shore. As is true elsewhere, inlets are the best bets.

When you reach the Lake Worth waters at Palm Beach, you have hit the best bluefishing in Florida. Tony Accetta, founder of the lure company that bears his name, used to try new designs on both large and small blues here and would discard models that did poorly. By fishing many lines at one time, he could get an excellent comparative picture among various lures used.

Trolling deep, particularly in the vicinity of Peanut Island, produces well. Night fishing on the full moon is considered optimum, yet blues of all sizes, from snappers to those in the 20-pound bracket, are taken even during daylight. Casting also should not be neglected.

The inlet area at Boynton Beach has long been famous for runs of huge jack crevalle. When they come inshore, bluefish often are mingled with them. Bait fish suffer: anglers do not. From this point down through Miami to Cape Florida Light, there is also some fishing inshore for small specimens. However, along the Florida Keys, bluefish must be considered a minor species and catches are incidental when after other game.

Rounding the tip of Florida to the Gulf of Mexico, another basic stock of bluefish predominates and fish do not reach the size of their Atlantic relatives. From East Cape to Naples, the season is November and December in a normal year with another run in March. Between Naples and Clearwater, the season peaks a bit earlier during both the late fall and early spring runs.

Inshore, throughout most of Florida's Gulf of Mexico side, and often on the close-in offshore waters, bluefish arrive in the spring, usually in late March or early April. As the season progresses, they school along the coasts of Alabama, Mississippi, Louisiana, and the northern coast of Texas. Freshwater run-off from the river systems, however, may drive them away from the beaches. Taken by both shore casters and boatmen, they are often found in the same areas as Spanish mackerel.

Gulf blues are not a separate species although all of those beached or boated in semitropical waters are lighter in color than their counterparts in the cold north. This undoubtedly is a normal change of coloration due to environment—a common thing among many fishes. The northern seas are gray-green while those of the Gulf salt water are powder-blue. The fish are simply adapting their own camouflage to their surroundings. Note also that this race of fish evidently can tolerate water temperatures considerably warmer than those found along the Atlantic coast. This adaptation to the searing heat of a Gulf summer apparently is necessary for survival. In addition, it may account for a reduced growth rate.

Earlier in this book, I have listed the general world-wide range of bluefish and have highlighted some of the better spots outside the waters of the United States. It is not my intention to give a port-by-port rundown of foreign fishing areas even though, in some locations such as Australia, these hot spots are well known. I think it is unlikely that the inhabitants of Morocco or the Azores will stampede in their rush to the bookstores to see whether or not I have included their favorite fishing grounds. For those who wish to try their bluefishing luck outside of the United States, study the first part of this chapter. Then make friends with the necessary foreigners.

Good bluefishing water is much the same the world over. The trick is to recognize it.

3

Trolling, Still Fishing and Jigging Tackle

When estimating the value of anglers' fishes by the play they give, and the scene into which the angler is led in search of each kind, the blue-fish must occupy a foremost rank; and the man who has neither trolled nor still-baited for this peculiar fish—the best breakfast fish on our coast except for the Spanish mackerel—has two treats in store, which, the sooner he improves, the earlier he will regret that he had not tasted before.

So wrote Genio C. Scott in his classic *Fishing in American Waters*, published in 1875. His tackle consisted of a cotton hand-line, a stout leader, an artificial lure or natural bait, and his hands, clothed in heavy cotton gloves since "buckskin or dogskin . . . are only a momentary protection," served in place of a reel. Scott would be amazed today to see the developments in modern fishing tackle. It is odd, however, that he never sought bluefish with rod and reel, for he used this combination often when after striped bass and weakfish.

RODS

Materials used in the manufacture of trolling rods, which may be used also for still fishing and jigging, were not dreamed of in Scott's day. At the end of World War II, glass fibers bonded with various types of resin took over from bamboo and other natural woods. These first glass rods were expensive, basically because experimentation was continuing to overcome difficulties experienced when the tackle was subjected to heavy strain. The early models at times literally exploded with the subsequent loss of fish and possible injury to the angler. However, research and development soon overcame these difficulties. In addition, competition in the marketplace brought down prices so that costs were affordable for the average fisherman.

So-called solid glass rods today are made from fibers which usually are of larger diameter towards the butt end and taper gradually to the tip. The fibers are then bonded together, fittings mounted and the whole works assembled to produce the finished product. Such rods are in the lower price range and are often standard equipment for party boats on which inexperienced anglers may well submit tackle to excessive wear and tear. Solid glass tends to have a fairly stiff action, which actually can be an advantage when jigging with heavy lures. The material will take a great deal of punishment and, with proper care, will last for years.

Weight and stiffness of solid glass rods make them perfectly adequate for many types of fishing, yet they are less than ideal for casting. Almost simultaneously, several companies developed the hollow glass method of manufacture in which glass fibers are woven together, wrapped around a core or mandrel, bonded and cured to produce a tapered blank, hollow at the center. Methods of making such rods are legion. Wall thickness, taper, bonding resins and all the rest now make almost any type of action available. Addition of graphite, then boron, to the hollow glass manufacturing process adds another dimension in fine-tuning of rod action and will be covered in the chapter on casting tackle. Hollow glass rods lead the popularity list among bluefishermen who do not concentrate on casting.

Hollow glass has an advantage as far as ferrules are concerned. Metal ferrules add weight to a rod, interrupt smooth action and have a tendency to bind and even corrode. Today, better-quality rods have glass-to-glass connections in two or more piece models. However, a metal ferrule between the butt end of the tip section and the butt itself is still standard in trolling rods. It is also standard in popping rods, which are single-handed, light tackle models with a straight butt that may be used for many types of fishing.

With regard to rod butts, note that standard big game trolling rods, which in lighter models may be used for bluefishing, all have a gimbal nock at the base of the butt. This seats into a gimbal fitting on the fighting chair. Boat rod butts on the other hand terminate in a rubber or plastic cap that is normally held against the body. The latter are preferred when after bluefish since the angler has more maneuverability in the cockpit and when bringing a hooked fish alongside.

REELS

When it comes to reels for trolling, jigging and still fishing, free-spool models should be the choice. For years, such reels were called "conventional," but conventions have changed and spinning reels have taken over in the casting arena. Certainly, spinning outfits may be used for trolling and the like, but these reels are designed primarily for casting. Free-spool models give more control in presenting a lure, in controlling it with or without a fish attached, and are more rugged in construction. Metal spools should be selected rather than plastic, again because they are rugged. The lightness of the plastic spool is an advantage when casting only. Metal is an absolute necessity when using wire line.

Unfortunately, reel manufacturers have never agreed on the standardization of numerals to indicate various sizes and line ca-

Typical free-spool reels. From top, clockwise, heavy trolling, wire line trolling, two standard surf casting reels, light casting reel. Photo by Hal Lyman.

pacities of their products. A 4/0 is larger than a 3/0 in the same company's catalog, but there accurate comparisons stop. Tabulation of the various types and yardage of line a particular reel will hold now is given in catalogs and in the literature describing the tackle, so reel capacity has evolved as the basic criterion of size.

With few exceptions, salt water reels today are equipped with a drag mechanism, which is nothing more than a type of adjustable brake which allows pressure to be put on a fish when it is taking off line. A lever, button or other device permits the angler to disengage this brake while letting out line so that the reel spool spins without restraint other than that applied by the human thumb—hence the name free-spool. Normally salt water reels also feature an anti-reverse lock which prevents the reel's handle from spinning backwards. In early ocean angling, there was no such mechanism and the term "knuckle-duster" or "knuckle-buster" was aptly applied. A smooth drag is one of the first characteristics to look for when selecting a reel.

Since the speed at which the lure moves through the water is set by the boat for the troller and, on the horizontal plane, may be considered zero when still fishing or jigging, gear ratio of a reel for such fishing is based primarily on that which is best for fighting a hooked blue. Most such reels feature a ratio between two and three to one—that is, one turn of the reel handle will rotate the spool two or three times.

For those who do not have an educated left thumb to spool line smoothly on the retrieve, many salt water fishing reels, particularly in models that have a line capacity of about 300 yards or less, incorporate a level wind device which is activated when the reel handle is turned. This prevents line from piling up at one point on the spool so that it jams against the crossbars. Level wind reels have their place when trolling or still fishing, but I do not favor them when jigging. Sudden tension, then slack in the line often throws mysterious half-hitches between spool and level wind itself in a manner that, to me, defies the laws of physics. Results can be disastrous.

LINE

Line has come a long way from the old days of tarred cotton and twisted linen. As was the case with glass fiber, major developments in synthetics burgeoned after World War II. Braided nylon was the first to appear and, to be honest, those early lines stretched almost as much as a rubber band. To set a hook when 50 yards or more had been streamed was a major undertaking. In addition, as is true of monofilament, the line has what is termed "memory." After a fish has been fought and the line has been rewound on the reel, it contracts to its former molecular structure. In those early days, that force often would rupture the side plates on a reel spool. Much of this problem has been overcome, yet the stretch factor and the comparatively large diameter of the braid in higher pound tests means that it is favored primarily below the 50-pound class.

The E.I. duPont de Nemours and Company, Incorporated—known to all and sundry today simply as duPont—then developed another polyester fiber which carries the trade name of Dacron. This braid has less stretch than the equivalent in nylon, is of smaller diameter and is very tough. This makes it a good choice for trolling and jigging. Various companies have treated Dacron in various ways. For example, the Cortland Line Company produces a line called Micron, which is a coated Dacron braided in very small diameter. It works well when maximum line capacity is desired in a small reel and, incidentally, is ideal for fly-line backing.

Monofilament itself was the reason for the boom in spinning after the end of World War II. Early European spinning reels were filled with fine braided silk line. The twists and tangles I threw into such lines in my youth could have best been cleared with a blowtorch. Mono has not only taken over in the field of spinning, but is well on its way to doing the same in the free-spool area, up to and including big game fishing.

A tremendous amount of research has gone into the development of a wide range of monofilaments. Characteristics vary from very limp to very stiff. From colors of fluorescent orange and purple to no color at all, from very cheap to comparatively expensive. You pay your money and you take your choice. As is the case with all fishing tackle, make the choice in favor of quality produced by a manufacturer who will stand behind his product.

Cheap mono may vary in diameter within a single spool of line, has poor tensile and knot strength, and often is mislabeled. One sharpie dealer we know made it a practice to label his 20-pound test as 15-pound. When a fisherman shooting for an IGFA record brought this to his attention, he said: "What are you worried about? It's the strongest 15-pound test on the market!"

As far as mono line color is concerned, every major manufacturer has done a great deal of research in this area to come up with monofilaments of various shades, fluorescent and otherwise. The goal is to make such line visible to the fisherman so that tangles when several lines are streamed astern may be avoided, yet have the line invisible to the fish. Again, the angler takes his choice, but bluefishermen should avoid fluorescent blue or purple. Under bright sunlight conditions, blues at times will attack the line itself. Perhaps they feel that the line is a form of spaghetti dinner. No one knows for sure.

When filling a free-spool reel, mono that is slightly stiffer than that used for spinning is to be preferred. Loops of very limp line will cut down into the reel spool when under the strain of fighting a bluefish with a break often resulting. As previously noted, be sure the reel used is designed for mono due to its "memory" factor. Many use 50 yards or so of Dacron as backing to minimize any such trouble.

For the deep troller, single strand stainless steel or Monel alloy lines are used all along the bluefishing front. At this writing, the IGFA does not allow use of such lines in establishing world record catches, but approval is being seriously considered. For all practical purposes, 25-pound test wire is heavy enough for bluefishing. Charter skippers favor heavier metal simply because many of their clients may be amateurs who will break off lighter stuff. Wire, since it has no stretch, is unforgiving when battling a fish. Normally, a shot of 50 yards of wire at the most, backed with Dacron or other braid, will do the job.

A special outfit should be set aside for wire line fishing. A reel with a metal spool narrower than those found on standard trolling models makes handling of the wire, particularly on the retrieve, easier. Roller guides and tiptop on the rod used are needed because wire will groove other types of guides in short order.

A compromise of sorts when going deep may be made by using lead-cored line. This is a nylon or Dacron braid woven over a center of flexible lead wire. It is bulky and does not cut down through the water as rapidly as single strand wire, but it is far easier to handle. In addition, a reel filled with lead-core may be substituted very quickly for another carrying regular braid or mono without fear of damage to the rod guides.

Moving down the line towards the hook, the next item of tackle to be considered is the leader. Because of those chopping teeth of a bluefish, wire of some sort is favored among most fishermen. Single strand stainless steel undoubtedly leads the list. Note that blued or dull finish should be selected because often a hooked blue will be freed by one of its voracious companions striking at moving shiny wire. Leader wire strength is measured by gauge as indicated in the accompanying table.

Gauge Number	Diameter	Breaking Strain in Pounds
1	.010	20
2	.011	27
3	.012	32
4	.013	38
5	.014	44
6	.016	58
7	.018	69
8	.020	86
9	.022	104
10	.024	120
11	.026	140
12	.029	165

From the practical fishing point of view, the actual breaking strain of higher gauge numbers is comparatively unimportant, for no angler, using balanced tackle, could put enough pressure on the largest blue that swims to part such a leader. What *is* important is whether or not a bluefish can bite through the wire. A hooked fish, if allowed any slack, often will chomp through the leader by doubling back towards the fisherman. As noted above, one of its fellows may take a swipe at the wire. If the hook has been engulfed beyond the eye, the quarry keeps its jaws chattering madly and will cut itself free. Finally, a strong leader can assist in swinging the catch aboard or hoisting it onto a pier when no net or gaff is available.

Some years ago, I ran some experiments on a blue of about five pounds concerning its wire-cutting abilities. Holding lengths of various leaders crosswise in its mouth, I found that gauges up to and including #4 would be severed cleanly. A bad crimp was put in #5, but it was not cut. I therefore suggest #6 as minimum and personally favor #9 to give extra insurance against the onslaughts of real jumbos. Fortunately, no one was watching me during this experiment or they might have called for the men in white.

Obviously leaders should be matched with the over-all tackle being used. I personally favor a short length, perhaps not more than a foot, since it is easy to handle. In any case, it should not be longer than the rod for such long leaders are awkward when a fish is alongside. In addition, a heavy leader kills lure action to some degree. Water conditions also must be taken into account. Although blues rarely are leader shy, they may be when the ocean is clear and the sun is bright.

Bluefishermen today are not limited to single strand wire as a leader material. Twisted cable is manufactured with very small diameter and high tensile strength. This same cable coated with nylon provides a material of flexibility equal to regular cable, has less tendency to kink, and may be knotted. Even a length of very heavy nylon may be used, although I prefer better insurance against the force of bluefish teeth. Finally, if the lure is comparatively long, as in the case of a large spoon or metal jig, it is possible to take blues with no leader at all, for the lure itself acts as a buffer against those snapping jaws. Examine the upper set of teeth on a big blue after it has been caught on such lures. Those needle-like choppers will be worn down to the gum line.

There are all sorts of rigs modified to suit various circumstances. When fishing in a chum line, for example, a wire leader only about three inches long may be snelled to the hook shank. Those who swing their catch aboard may use about three feet of 40-pound monofilament between the running line and a foot-long wire leader. A special light tackle wire line trolling technique involves about 100 feet of mono joined to the line with a swivel small enough to pass through tiptop and guides, and with a normal wire leader at its terminal end. When trolling, mono and sufficient wire to reach the desired depth is streamed. When a fish is hooked, the wire is recovered as rapidly as possible and the blue may then be played primarily on the softer line.

My feelings about a clutter of snaps and swivels on any type of leader are strong. In my early bluefishing days, the standard leader sold by tackle shops had a heavy brass swivel at one end

Improved Clinch Knot

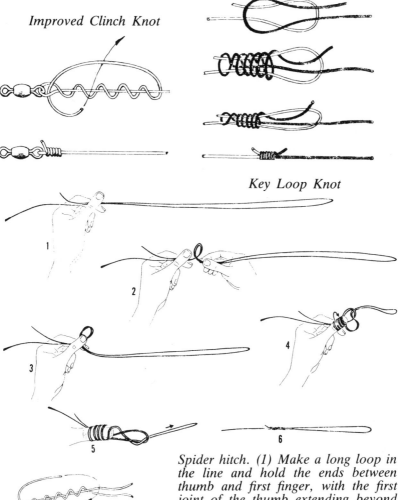

Key Loop Knot

Spider hitch. (1) Make a long loop in the line and hold the ends between thumb and first finger, with the first joint of the thumb extending beyond the finger as shown. (2) Use your other hand to twist a smaller reverse loop in the double line. (3) Slide the fingers up the line to hold the loop securely, with most of the loop extending beyond the tip of the thumb. (4) Wind the double line from right to left around both the thumb and the loop, taking five turns. Then pass what remains of the large loop through the small one. (5) Pull the large loop to make five turns unwind off the thumb. Use a fast, steady pull—not a quick jerk. Pull the turns around the base of the loop up tightly and snip off the protruding ends of the line.

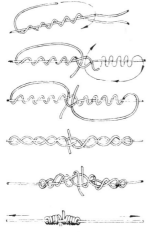

Blood Knot

and an even heavier snap swivel at the other. The bright brass was an invitation to bluefish not hooked and they would often free their companion by chomping on it. A small, dark swivel at the line end of a single strand wire leader makes tying-in of the line easy. A simple snap of the locking type at the terminal end facilitates changing lures. With nylon-covered cable, which I prefer over regular cable wire alone, line may be tied in with a key loop, thus dispensing with the swivel entirely. A crimped sleeve will do the same type of connecting job when regular cable wire is used.

Incidentally, when knots themselves are considered, I am not of the school that puts every knot used on the testing scale. The improved clinch works well for attaching line to a swivel or snap. If you want a double line for several feet above the leader, the Spider hitch is simple and strong. The blood knot is standard when joining two strengths of line together. A simple figure-of-eight does the trick when securing nylon-covered cable to a swivel or snap. If my line is going to break, I want it to break close to the terminal tackle—namely, at the knot. Hopefully, this will never happen when playing a fish, but it may well happen when fast to an underwater piece of real estate. It is better to lose a bit of terminal tackle than half a hundred yards of line along with said terminal gear. The exception to this rule is when employing a very light outfit when every ounce of strength counts.

HOOKS

At the end of a leader in one form or another is the fundamental connection between the angler and his quarry—the hook. Although this item is extremely important to fishing success, an incredible number of anglers will scrimp and save a few pennies when buying a hook while they think nothing of spending many dollars just to reach the seashore. Investment in the best hooks available is a small one as far as cash flow is concerned, but is prime security when the battle with a bluefish is joined.

Any fishhook is a compromise of sorts between the hook's

ability to penetrate and its ability to hold once it has penetrated. Basically, if the bite of the hook—that portion extending from the bottom of the bend to the point—is short, it will penetrate easily, but may not hold well. If the bite is long, the reverse in general is true. Over the years, the most popular styles used by bluefishermen have been the O'Shaughnessy and the Eagle Claw type. The latter is particularly popular when still fishing with natural bait. The Siwash, which originated on the Pacific Coast, is another type that comes in a poor third in ranking.

As far as hook sizes are concerned, much depends upon the tackle used and the weight of fish expected. For example, it would be impractical to terminate a light popping rod outfit with a 6/0 hook when after snappers, yet such a hook would cause no problem when used with a stout boat rod in waters holding jumbos. Anything larger than a 6/0 for bluefishing is unnecessary, for it is difficult to set the hook and, once set, it tends to buttonhole. This means simply that the hook metal wears through the flesh of the fish to make a gap through which the barb may pass. When a bluefish jumps and shakes its head, button-holing is a real cause for concern—at least for the fisherman. A 2/0 is normally the smallest practical size when trolling, still fishing or jigging.

When selecting hook sizes and styles, attention should be given also to the diameter of the wire from which the hook is made. In general, salt water hooks are graded in ascending wire sizes as follows: regular, strong, X strong, XX strong, and so on

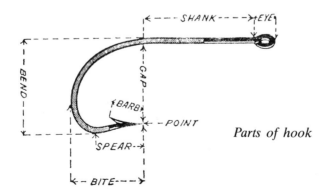

Parts of hook

up to five X's. For all practical purposes, X or XX strong of regular rounded wire are heavy enough for bluefishing. If forged—that is with the hook bend hammered flat—an X strong hook will hold any blue I have caught to date.

Material from which the hook is made is important. High quality tempered steel, cadmium plated and tinned, leads the list. Such hooks hold their point sharpness well, but touching them up with a file, honing stone or silicon carbide sandpaper will improve their penetration effectiveness. They stand up under pressure, are not brittle and, eventually, will rust. When a hook rusts, get rid of it. Cost of replacement is minimal. Blued, so-called bronzed, Japanned and similar lacquered hooks, allegedly designed for salt water use, should be avoided. They corrode all too quickly. Gold plated specimens are used by many anglers fishing with natural bait since the gold color itself is an attractor.

Development of stainless steel hooks has come a long way since the early experiments with a wide variety of such alloys. Trying to reach an engineering compromise between metals that were too soft or too brittle took many years, but today all major manufacturers produce stainless models which, although not basically as strong in equivalent wire diameters as tempered steel, are highly satisfactory. Note also that the price tag on stainless hooks is higher than that of the tinned variety. Stainless is favored on lures dressed with feathers or synthetic materials because there is no discoloration from rust.

BALANCING TACKLE

From hooks to rods, reels and lines, balanced tackle is a necessity for successful bluefishing. The outfits I am about to describe are for *practical* use. Heavier gear may be used by those whose only interest is in filling the fish box. Conversely, lighter tackle may be used by those trying to establish a record on gossamer line—attempts which may be defined as stunt fishing. Balanced tackle, incidentally, does not mean that the weight of reel and rod butt offsets the weight of the rod tip exactly. It means that all components of the outfit are matched for maximum efficiency and sport in hooking, playing and landing a fish.

In early salt water sport fishing days, trolling outfits were classified be the weight and length of the wooden rod tip, the length of the rod butt, and the thread count of linen line used. With the advent of synthetics, this system went by the board and classifications are made on the breaking strain of the line in accordance with IGFA record categories. The heaviest of these normally used for bluefishing is the 50-pound outfit. Although it is heavier than required, many charter and party boat skippers have it as standard because they know that some of their clients will break anything lighter—and a boat captain does not appreciate losing expensive terminal gear because of ignorance or misuse.

For record purposes, the IGFA requires that a rod tip must be 40 inches in length as a minimum and the butt must not exceed 27 inches. These limits do not apply to either surf casting or fly fishing tackle. Even when not seeking records, the limits make sense and do away with stubby or freak outfits.

For bluefishing, a balanced 50-pound outfit consists of a reel holding 250 yards or more of monofilament, nylon or Dacron; rod tip length, no less than five feet, and rod butt approximately 18 inches. For jigging, as contrasted with trolling or still fishing, tip action should be fairly stiff. Today fortunately all major tackle manufacturers list in their catalogs just which rod matches which reel and line. As previously noted, if wire line is to be used with this outfit or any other listed below, roller guides and tiptop are to be preferred.

More suited to bluefishing is the 30-pound rig with a reel holding approximately 350 yards of this test line. Rod tip and butt measurements are the same as in the 50-pound outfit, but naturally the tip is lighter and has more limber action. Below 30-pound test line, IGFA categories in pounds are 20, 16, 12, 8, 4 and 2. For practical purposes when trolling, jigging or still fishing, anything less than 8-pound must be considered in the stunt fishing category and even 8-pound with a free-spool reel verges on the borderline. Ignoring IGFA, I often choose 10-pound for

Typical free-spool trolling tackle produces a typical bluefish on an underwater plug. Photo by Barry Gibson.

light tackle work.

Choices among balanced outfits to suit these line tests are legion. I do not plan to list them all here, but again recommend manufacturers' catalogs. There are some general rules for selection, however. For pier and bridge fishermen, tackle must be sturdy enough to hoist a flapping bluefish through the air during the tail end of the battle. Similarly, a party boat angler will make nothing but enemies if his gear is so light that the blue entangles lines on all sides while the fish swims out of control. Finally, when considering reel capacities of any test line selected, err on the plus side. Nothing is more frustrating when expecting small blues than to have a 20-pounder hit, run off all the line and snap it at the reel arbor.

For still fishing from a boat or land-based structure, there is one outfit that is neither balanced, standardized, lovely to look at, nor expensive. It is efficient. Youngsters over the years have used it to capture snappers and it is splendid tackle to introduce kids to the sport. The outfit is simple: a long Chinese, Japanese, or even domestic bamboo pole, a length of line secured to its tip, and a baited hook. Even children barely able to toddle can handle such gear with considerable success.

With the exception of the cane pole outfit, too much emphasis cannot be placed upon buying quality tackle when selecting a balanced outfit. Certainly there are times when bargain sales provide opportunity to save money, but be sure that the bargain is a financial one and does not depend upon shoddy merchandise being substituted for advertised quality. *Caveat emptor*—let the buyer beware—is as sound advice today as it was a thousand years ago.

4

Casting Tackle

Casters tend to be a trifle smug when they compare their method of fishing to that of trollers. They claim that anyone can drag a lure or bait through the water with the boat doing the work, but that it takes real skill to present an offering tossed through the air so that it gets results. There is a modicum of truth in such an attitude which, in an odd way, has spread to the selection of the tackle itself. Specialization has caused development of so many types of casting combinations, as compared with the few general types used when trolling, that rod and reel manufacturers rub their hands in glee.

Even the august IGFA has had to make adjustments in its world record eligibility rules to accomodate surf fishermen, who form a special group among casters. "Rods must comply with sporting ethics and customs," the regulations read, but unlike the case with other categories of tackle, there are no restrictions on actual measurements. However, from the practical point of view, there are what might be termed self-imposed restrictions. The belief that the longer the rod, the longer the cast does not stand up under scrutiny. Physical build and power of the angler concerned must be taken into account along with his casting technique and skill.

No matter what type of surf casting tackle is used, the angler is overgunned for the quarry he seeks. The reason is simple: the

The author leans into a cast from the beach at Orleans on Cape Cod. Photo by Frank Woolner.

lure or bait must be tossed far enough into the ocean to reach the fish. In addition, the rod must be long enough to keep the line above the crest of breaking waves pounding in on the beach. With the advent of synthetic materials that replaced bamboo, today's surf rods have sufficient flexibility to make playing a hooked bluefish a sporting event. Some distance casters favor very stiff blanks, but these club-like rods result in many hooks tearing loose from a bluefish's jaws.

The high surf outfit is a specialty weapon designed to cast lures or bait and sinker combinations from three to six or more ounces for long distances in rugged water. It is at its optimum when using three-to five-ounce weights. For best results, the rod should be a one-piece job, which admittedly is difficult to transport. For the average angler, overall length should not exceed 11 feet plus a few inches and the 10½ footer is a normal standard. Glass fiber, graphite and boron models are all available with the last two, used by those reaching the expert level in distance casting, more costly.

To match such rods, select a free-spool reel holding a minimum of 250 yards of 25 to 30-pound braided line or 20- to 25-pound monofilament. In former times, high surf addicts often opted for 45-pound test when night fishing, but such extra strength really is not needed. However, a shock line five to ten pounds heavier than the running line is recommended. This is a length of heavier monofilament tied into the running line to absorb shock on the cast. It should be long enough to reach from the leader to two or three turns around the reel spool.

Note that free-spool casting reels are wider than their trolling equivalents so that there is less inertia to overcome. The spool itself should be light in weight, either plastic or light metal alloy. Many surf men favor the comparatively new designs which have built-in magnetic controls to minimize backlashes. The Penn Mag Power and Daiwa Magforce series are typical. An educated thumb should be substituted for the standard level-wind mechanism on a surf reel since the latter not only cuts down on casting distance, but also fouls all too readily on a sandy beach. The retrieve ratio in gears is a matter of personal preference. The

Penn Squidder series, long a favorite among surf casters, has a ratio of 3½ to 1 while the Jigmaster can be bought with as high as a 5 to 1 ratio for speedy retrieve. If such a model is selected, it is wise to fill the spool with at least 30-pound test because the shock of the strike, when the fish may be moving rapidly in one direction while the lure is moving in the other, may snap lighter line.

Turning to spinning, there are certain characteristics which should be taken into account when chosing a reel for bluefishing. First, it should be a model designed for salt water use since fresh water reels will soon jam and corrode away in the briny. The drag mechanism must be both smooth and tough. It is here that many spinning reels fall down. I personally do not care whether the drag control is on the face of the spool, at the rear of the reel housing, or elsewhere as long as it will operate properly and will not back off or tighten up under its own power. In brief, once I set the drag, I want it to stay set until I choose to change it.

Positive bail action is also important. This means that the bail will close firmly to pick up the line when the reel handle is turned and will *not* close of its own accord on the cast. Some anglers have become so unhappy with faulty bails that they cut them off and pick up the line manually on the retrieve. Fortunately such extreme measures have become less common in recent years as manufacturers perfected their products. Still, however, I and countless other anglers have been caught far away from any tackle store with a broken bail spring. The bail itself hangs like a broken gull's wing and, if there is no replacement spring handy, fishing may come to a stop. Spare springs should be standard items in the spinning anglers kit.

The high surf spinning outfit as far as a rod is concerned is much the same as that selected for use with a free-spool reel. However, the rod itself normally is of more limber action, particularly near the tip. Use of a thumb stall is to be recommended to save wear and tear of the index finger on the cast. The reel should hold roughly 300 yards of 20-pound mono. I do not favor dropping below that weight, although some seeking casting distance may disagree. The outfit is designed for heavy lures or bait and sinker combinations, so lighter line will deteriorate rapidly. Heat, which is generated particularly when starting a cast, has a bad effect upon monofilament.

A few years ago, spinning with a high surf outfit took over along almost all coasts and those using free-spool reels, myself included, were considered something of an anachronism. The pendulum now appears to have swung the other way as anglers find that they have more control of heavy lures and baits, of a fish after it is hooked, and even of pinpoint accuracy in high winds when a free-spool reel is used. There is also no question that free-spool models can stand more physical punishment than spinning equivalents.

The standard surf outfit handles weights from about two to four ounces, measures nine to ten feet overall, and mounts a free-spool reel holding at least 200 yards of 25- to 30-pound braided line or 20- to 25-pound monofilament. Its equivalent in spinning may have a rod six inches longer with a reel capacity of about 250 yards of 12- to 15-pound mono. Heavier line may be used if desired, but will cut down distance on the cast. In general, anglers using spinning gear should choose lines somewhat lighter than their free-spool brethren. The reason: friction builds up at the edge of a spinning reel spool as line goes out and this friction is less as the diameter of the line on the reel spool decreases.

Next down the line in size is what is termed a squidding or jetty jockey outfit which handles weights from slightly more than an ounce up to those of three ounces. Ideal for jetty fishing and boat casting when the going is rough, overall rod length is about eight feet and the reel should hold a minimum of 150 yards of 12- to 15-pound braid or mono. The spinning equivalent again may be six inches longer as far as the rod is concerned with the reel holding roughly 250 yards of 10- or 12-pound test. Accuracy rather than distance is the goal of this combination.

All the above are two-handed casting outfits and as noted I favor a free-spool reel for them. However, my loyalties change when it comes to what may be considered the most versatile, all-purpose casting tackle combination under a wide variety of circumstances in single-handed category. This is a spinning rod approximately eight feet overall mounting a reel holding between 200 and 250 yards of 8- to 10-pound mono. This rig will handle lures from the tiny midgets of a half-ounce up to a strong two ounces. It serves well for casting from both small and large craft, from shores of tidal rivers and estuaries—in fact from any area where blues may be found within a 50-yard radius in deep or shallow water.

The free-spool equivalent is a sea-going bait-casting rod—known in the old days as a weakfish model—with a tip no less than five feet in length and an extension butt which may be braced against the midriff when battling a hooked blue. This butt, about 18 inches long, should mount a reel holding at least 150 yards of a 12- to 15-pound test braid or monofilament. Such a combination handles lures a trifle heavier than the spinning rig and is to be preferred if trolling as well as casting is involved. The popping rod, which is also excellent for bluefishing, is similar, but the rod tip may be as long as six feet. This outfit is a favorite among pier and bridge fishermen if the catch does not have to be derricked up from the water surface.

Lighter tackle combinations of course may be used, particularly when the angler is fairly certain that only small blues are in evidence—a condition that cannot be anticipated regularly. I rarely drop the line test below the 8-pound mark. Fly fishing involves a completely different type of tackle which will be covered in the chapter that follows.

Concerning monofilament lines for spinning, many tend to over-emphasize the need for limpness. It certainly is true that you do not want a stiff and springy line when spinning, or when using any other type of reel for that matter. However, excessive limpness will result in line sloughs—loops of line pulled off the reel spool in a tangle. Selection is a matter of personal preference, but extremes should be avoided.

Terminal tackle for the caster varies considerably from that used by the troller. A long wire leader, even when fishing with a high surf outfit, causes trouble since it cannot pass through the rod tiptop at the start of a cast without jamming. With two-handed surf rods, an 18-inch leader of blued stainless wire, cable or nylon-covered cable is long enough. With lighter tackle, leader length should be reduced to half that, or less. A simple locking snap at one end of the leader makes lure changing easy and a small barrel swivel at the other end serves as a connecting point to the line by means of an improved clinch knot. Bait fishermen dispense with the snap since the hook is tied into the leader itself.

When casting light lures, any sort of wire leader tends to alter, or even kill completely, action of the lure itself. Therefore it is wise to keep leader lengths at a reasonable minimum. This leader disadvantage is especially true when fishing with small, surface-swimming plugs.

Obviously the purpose of a wire leader is to prevent blues from biting through the softer line. When a shock line is used and when large lures, such as tinclads or big plugs, are cast, there is really no reason to add anything other than a locking snap at the end of the shock. Those snapping teeth will expend their energy on the lure itself to the detriment of both teeth and lure. However, if the lure is small enough to be swallowed by the fish or if natural bait is employed, wire of some sort is recommended.

One rig that the surfman using bait should have in his tackle bag is the fishfinder. This device is similar to a sliding sinker, but the "slide" traveling along the line is separated from the sinker. Fishfinders come in various designs, both of metal and of plastic. I opt for the metal models since they stand up almost forever. A regular swivel, which cannot pass through the eye of the fishfinder, checks the sinker during the cast. When the sinker reaches bottom, leader, hook and bait are clear of any weight so the slightest nibble is relayed to the rod tip. Although blues are voracious, there are times when they will toy with a bait and, if they feel sinker weight, as is the case when no fishfinder is used, they will drop the hook, never to return. The fishfinder user lowers his rod tip under such conditions to give a bit of slack, then strikes when the blue starts to take off.

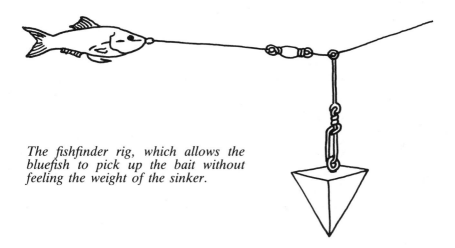

The fishfinder rig, which allows the bluefish to pick up the bait without feeling the weight of the sinker.

In the previous chapter, I discussed terminal tackle in some detail. The same comments apply in general to those using casting outfits, but there are a few exceptions. Hook sizes, except in the case of those using two-handed rods while bait fishing, should be smaller than those favored by trollers. Tackle is lighter and it is difficult to set a hook much larger than a 2/0 with the 8-foot spinning combination described earlier. Many light artificial lures feature hooks even smaller. Note that, in these smaller sizes, the hook wire should be far heavier than that commonly found on freshwater plugs. A black bass among the lilypads does not have the crushing power in its jaws which characterize a bluefish.

For many years, the IGFA did not recognize for a world record any fish taken on a plug rigged with a series of hooks. As casting with standard plugs, which often have as many as three trebles attached, became more and more popular among sea-going anglers, the rules were changed. Today no more than three hooks, treble, double, single of a combination of all three, attached to any artificial lure designed for their use, are approved. In point of fact, a clutter of hooks on a plug or other artificial may be a disadvantage when after bluefish. The fish may spend considerable effort fighting the lure itself and using leverage against it to tear loose. If balance of a plug is not affected seriously, it often pays to cut off the middle treble in a lure that features three, or cut off the leading treble in one that carries only two.

Casters offering natural bait to blues should select sinkers with some care. A pyramid sinker, for example, is ideal when the beach is smooth and sandy. It will bury in the ocean floor and not roll about as a bank sinker would. On rock-studded or shell bottom, the pyramid will foul regularly while the bank will slip free of most obstacles. Unfortunately there is no sinker design that will never foul bottom at all. As this is being written, the Cape Cod Canal in Massachusetts is being dredged—and the Canal is prime bluefishing water. I am sure that some enterprising scavenger willing to sift through the mud and muck of the dredge spoil could coin a substantial amount of money by selling the recovered lead lost by anglers over many years.

If a bait fisherman frequents areas of rough bottom, such as the oyster shell beds found in many coastal sections south of the Mason-Dixon Line, he can economize by using small bags of sand in place of standard sinkers. These should be attached to terminal gear with heavy thread, which will break readily, leaving the sandbag behind. Bull Durham tobacco bags are often used for this type of expendable sinker.

I have just skimmed the surface of the many facets of casting for blues. Many books have been written on special aspects of casting itself, ranging from distance casting in the surf to specialized plugging in estuarine waters. I personally derive more pleasure casting for bluefish than trying to take them by other means. The sport combines both angling and hunting, plus a challenge in honing one's own skills. I have even been known to catch a fish from time to time using tackle designed for this task. More on this subject will be found in chapters that follow when methods are described.

5

Fly Fishing Tackle

Back in 1939, the late Harlan Major wrote a book, *Salt Water Fishing Tackle,* which was a classic of its time. An avid researcher and keen angler, Major delved into angling history and came up with facts which few had discovered previously. I quote his comments on the origin of the fly used for fishing:

> It was during the third century that the artificial fly was first specifically mentioned. Aelian (Claudius Aelianus, Roman author and rhetorician) speaking of Macedonian fishing, wrote that a fly called the Hippourus, which was not a bee though it hummed like one, was fed upon by a fish with "spotted fins" which swam in the river Astracus. The fly, however, was too delicate to impale on a hook as it would lose its color and decay as soon as touched. Thus the only fly these fish would take could not be used, and a substitute was made. "They fasten crimson red wool around a hook, and fit on the hook two feathers, which grow under a cock's wattle, and which in color is like wax."

I have never run into a Hippourus myself, but there is no question that the fishermen Aelian mentioned started something which has developed over centuries into a major advance in angling. Shelves of books have been written about fly fishing and, unfortunately, a mystique has gathered around this phase of the sport with the result that many feel that casting with a fly rod requires extraordinary skill verging on art. Such is not the case. It is easier to learn to cast a fly far enough to reach fish than it is to learn the same using a free-spool reel. Fly fishing for bluefish has come into its own in recent years.

One of the early pioneers in this angling arena was the late George Bonbright, who made a name for himself in fly fishing for tarpon in Florida during the early 1900s. He used to travel by dory to the tide rips off Great Point on Nantucket Island armed with a split bamboo, two-handed Atlantic salmon rod and large flies. Since outboard motors had not been invented, his means of propulsion was two stalwart oarsmen, who must have disliked bluefishing forever after.

Bonbright would stand in the dory while the rowers held the boat in position against the current. He could see bluefish through the clear water lying, as he said, "like lead pencils" in

Ted Lyman of Dover, Massachusetts, fights a blue on fly fishing tackle. Photo by H.K. Bramhall.

the rip. He reported that often on his first cast to a particular fish, there would be no indication that the blue had even seen the fly. On the second cast, the fish might stir. On the third, Bonbright would brace his feet, for a hit almost always followed. All of which indicates that it pays to make at least three casts over the same water no matter what tackle is used.

Fly casting falls into a special category. In all other types of casting, the weight of the lure draws line from the reel. The line itself and action of the rod is what propels the fly to its target. Timing by the caster is all-important and a neophyte may learn rudiments of the technique in a short time when coached by a fellow angler who knows the game. After basics have been mastered, then refinements, like the double-haul to increase distance, may be learned.

Balanced tackle is perhaps more important when fly fishing than in any other type of casting. An ill-matched rod, reel and line combination not only will result in poor casts as far as distance and accuracy are concerned, but also will cause excessive fatigue for the angler. Note particularly that, just because bluefish are found in the ocean, it does not mean that heavy outfits such as those used to subdue huge tarpon on tropical flats are required.

Concerning rods, after glass fiber construction took over from split bamboo on the ocean front, additions of first graphite, then boron, to the basic mix first started among manufacturers of fly rods. They were seeking rod actions that varied from those required to present a delicate dry fly in a mountain brook to tossing a ten-inch streamer to sailfish. In thumbing through rod catalogs today, it is obvious that they have succeeded. The variations in rod weights, lengths and actions are legion. For bluefishermen, salt water models are required. These are equipped with fittings and guides which are resistant to the corrosive action of sea water.

As a general rule, blanks with a major portion of graphite added in the mix are stiffer and more powerful than those made from fiberglass alone. This power and stiffness increases when boron is added. Actually "stiffness" is not quite the right term.

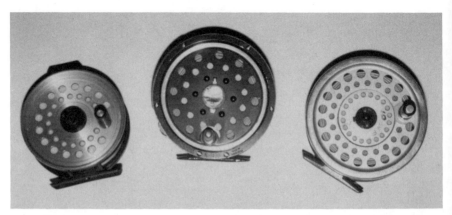

Typical fly reels, left to right, light, medium and heavy. Photo by Hal Lyman.

The graphite and boron models snap back to their original conformation quickly, but are still limber overall. One of the great enemies of the angler using fly fishing tackle for blues is wind. Graphite and boron models, while more expensive than fiberglass, can help defeat this.

Fly reels, with few exceptions, are single action. Most seagoing models are equipped with a drag mechanism. Frankly, I think too much emphasis is placed on such drags by many anglers seeking bluefish. Of course the drag should be smooth, but fancy gearing, levers and controls add both weight and expense. A drag set tightly enough to prevent a line over-run on the reel spool to me is sufficient. Added pressure, if required, may be given by hand, thumb or finger, depending upon the reel's construction. The fly reel's primary function is storage of line.

Modern fly lines are classified by number, plus letters to indicate the type of taper and whether the line is floating or sinking. Thus an L-7-F is a level, 7-weight, floating line and a WF-8-F/S is a weight forward, 8-weight, floating line with a sinking tip. Most saltwater fly fishermen, myself included, prefer weight-forward lines since they can be "shot" into the wind far more easily than level or double-taper types. Rarely, if ever, does a bluefisherman have to present a fly extremely delicately as his counterpart trying to match the evening hatch of mayflies on a trout stream is required to do.

Floating lines are the choice if popping bugs are the lures used, but normally a floating line with a sinking tip will do the job better when angling with regular streamers. In fast tide rips, a truly sinking line may be needed to get the hook down to the quarry. Such lines are a nuisance to use because they must be stripped in almost completely before casting again or else excessive strain is put on the rod tip. A spare reel spool, entire reel, or even a second complete outfit provide several choices.

A reel selected to balance with the rod chosen should hold not only a full length of fly line, but also a minimum of 75 yards of 20- to 25-pound test backing. Even more is preferred as insurance in case a monster is hooked. Although regular braided nylon or Dacron serves well as backing, Micron is the best choice due to its small diameter when compared to strength. Some sing the praises of the nail knot to join fly line and backing, but I have had unhappy experiences with that connector and prefer the key loop.

A well matched outfit for bluefishing consists of a fly rod measuring 8½ to 9 feet in length mounting a reel holding an 8-weight, weight-forward, sinking tip line, plus about 100 yards of backing. Such tackle may be a bit heavy for blues averaging less than five pounds, but remember that wind! If fishing is done primarily at the surf line where casting distance may be important, jump to a 9 to 9½ footer with a 9- or 10-weight line of the same weight forward type.

Fly fishing is not stunt fishing. Charles F. Waterman, angling sage of Deland, Florida, and fly fisherman extraordinary, wrote in *Salt Water Sportsman* back in 1986: "There are some cases where what sounds like the toughest may actually be the easiest. For example, on many fish the long fly rod is tolerant of tension mistakes and the fly reel is so simple there isn't much wrong to be done with it." Note that the large diameter fly line provides considerable resistance as it moves through the water. Coupled with the flex of the rod, which is superbly designed to absorb sudden shocks, a bluefish definitely does not have all the advantage.

Leaders present a special problem when fly fishing for blues.

Spider Andresen displays a fly rod catch. Note the extension butt on the rod, which may be braced against the body during the battle. Photo by Spider Andresen.

Even when long-shanked hooks are used, chances are that the fish will take the fly deep enough so that its teeth can chomp through a monofilament leader. A very heavy mono tippet is impossible to thread through the eye of a normal fly, so some sort of wire may be required. Weight of such metal makes casting difficult and I have yet to find the ideal solution.

Even the IGFA begs the question a bit. It permits a shock tippet of metal at the end of a standard leader, but the metal must not exceed 12 inches in length. For ease in casting, any metal shock tippet longer than four inches presents casting problems. The main trouble comes when trying to attach the fly to the wire. Diameter of nylon-covered cable of sufficient strength to prevent a bite-through will not go through the hook eye. Fine wire—gauges #1 through #4—overcome this difficulty, yet twisting such wire every time a fly is changed is awkward. In addition, a large bluefish can cut such fine diameter stainless all too easily. My compromise, which leaves a good deal to be desired, is four inches of #6 gauge wire tipped with a tiny snap. Such a rig impairs the fly's action to some degree, but it will have to do until something better comes along.

FLIES

In a later chapter, natural and artificial lures for fishing with tackle other than a fly rod will be discussed. However, since fly fishing really falls into a class by itself, let me take up flies and other tempters here and now.

Basically, there are two types of flies commonly used by blue-fishermen: the streamer and the popping bug. The former may be fished at almost any depth while the latter is a surface lure. There is no need to present fancily dressed offerings, such as some of the Atlantic salmon traditional flies. One bluefish catch will make mincemeat of the lure anyway! Bucktail, hackle feathers or crimped nylon fibers serve well for the wing. If hackle is used, I prefer it tied ahead of the wing itself since it gives an enticing "breathing" action to the fly. Fairly bulky bodies, usually of silver tinsel, are standard. A strip of Mylar for the cheek gives added flash. Hook sizes of #4 or #2 are large enough.

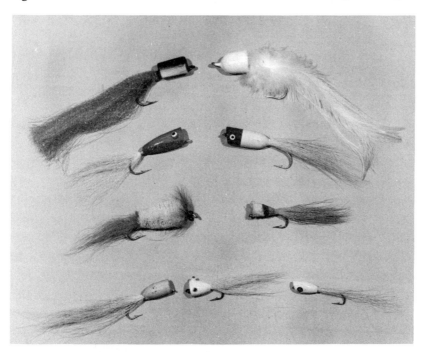

A variety of popping bugs and sliders, all of which will take bluefish.
Photo by Frank Woolner.

Color can range from plain white through all the primary colors and to coal black. Combinations of colors are endless and the angler should try to match in general the bait upon which blues are feeding. For example, when spearing are the prey, flies featuring white, yellow and silver should be the choice, but if small eels are serving as food, black and white streamers should be selected.

Long streamers tend to wrap around the hook bend on the cast. Paul Kukonen of Worcester, Massachusetts, fly caster and movie maker, solves this problem by tying a short tuft of bucktail *under* the streamer wing, which balances the wing itself high and tangle-free. The resulting fly is unlovely, but it works. Note also when using popping bugs plastic heads are better than cork and will take more punishment from bluefish teeth. The head should be concave to make as much surface fuss as possible when the fly is retrieved.

Retrieve itself can be all-important when bluefishing. With a popping bug, it should be erratic to simulate a wounded bait

Streamers and poppers, complete with bluefish, which will attack them.
Photo by Frank Woolner.

fish. When a regular streamer is used, however, speed often is the key to success. Stripping line in rapidly results in strikes when a more leisurely retrieve rate may produce nothing. If a blue swirls at a fly and misses, stop the retrieve momentarily to allow the fish time to turn around, then strip in line like crazy! Be sure that the stripped line does not become entangled in on shore obstructions or on the various cleats, knobs and edges found on any boat.

Fly fishing tackle may also be used to present natural baits . A tender morsel, such as a sandeel, is apt to tear off the hook when cast by any other outfit, yet can be flipped gently among feeding blues with a fly rod. This technique is especially useful when fishing in a chum slick. A small strip bait or even a sliver of pork rind may be substituted if an artificial fails to produce.

Some years ago, a group of bluefishermen developed such a technique to a fine point while fishing in the Cape Cod Canal in Massachusetts. Blues were gorging on sandeels and refused any other offering. Reels were loaded with standard backing to which was attached about 75 feet of 8- to 10-pound test monofilament. To the end of the mono was attached a short length of light wire, then a light hook. A netted sandeel was speared through the eye with the hook point.

Mono was stripped off the reel and coiled carefully into a basket belted around the angler's waist. A garbage pail lid at the fisherman's feet could be substituted. On the cast, the mono was clamped by hand against the rod handle and the bait was flipped through the air as when spinning. Distance casting obviously was not required. On the retrieve, the mono was coiled free of tangles into the basket. When the bluefish hit, they engulfed the bait, so there was no problem in setting the hook.

The trick during the battle is to get those coils of monofilament onto the reel without tangling. The first rush of the blue normally takes care of this. Fight the quarry with a pumping action of the rod, for mono has stretch that must be overcome. Today, a weighted shooting head such as those used by anglers seeking steelhead on the Pacific Coast can be substituted for the monofilament. The basic goal is to flip a soft bait without having it tear loose from the hook. This is a highly specialized use of fly fishing tackle, but it shows that such tackle is more versatile than many believe.

There are times when weather or the fish themselves conspire to make it difficult for a fly fisherman to cast far enough to reach the quarry. A sneaky trick to overcome such conditions is to have a companion, armed with long-range gear, cast a hookless plug to sighted blues. As he retrieves the lure, the fish will follow it and often whack it again and again. Their temper seems to increase in direct proportion with the number of times they fail to be caught. Enticed within fly casting range, the angler with the long wand can then go to work. A popping bug, dropped near the moving plug, usually will be gobbled down in short order.

The author fly casting for blues from a tide marsh bank. Photo by Frank Woolner.

'rank Woolner using a heavy fly rod for maximum distance casting in a tidal estuary.
hoto by Salt Water Sportsman.

One final word on fly fishing technique: when a bluefish jumps, keep the line taut. This goes against all the training and instincts of anglers brought up on the fresh water front and even of those who fish for tarpon in the briny with light tackle. The danger of a hooked fish falling back on the leader and breaking it is great in rivers, lakes and on tidal flats, so the time honored rule is: bow to a leaping fish. Bluefish, however, jump with much head-shaking in an attempt to dislodge the hook. Allowed the least bit of slack line, they will be successful. Chances of a thrown hook are far greater than those of a broken leader.

6

BAITS and LURES

Bluefish have the reputation of eating anything in the ocean that does not eat them first. They will even gobble down their own kind on occasion. Despite this ravenous appetite, there are times when the fish are unusually selective in their feeding habits, so an angler should be ready to shift offerings if the first one presented fails to produce.

BAITS

When the fish are finicky, I make it a practice to cut open the first one caught to discover what its natural diet of the moment may be. Then, if possible, I try to "match the hatch" as freshwater trout anglers say. In any fishing with natural bait, make sure that your own supply is as fresh as possible. Blues are not scavengers and like their meals firm and clean. A portable ice box or bucket is a good investment when fishing from a boat, pier or beach where considerable walking is not required. Live wells, of which there are many types ranging from portable units to those built into the hull, give boatmen an advantage by keeping herring, mullet and the like swimming naturally.

Crabs, which are favored by many bluefishermen south of the Mason-Dixon Line, will stay alive when packed loosely in seaweed. The same holds true of seaworms, although these wrigglers are costly and used primarily when after small fish. *Never* wet down such baits with fresh water, for they will die quickly.

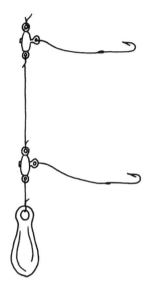

The High-Low rig allows baits to be presented at two different depths when still fishing or drifting.

If ice is used, have the baits suspended above it in a wire mesh rack. Eels, which will take large blues, particularly at night, are almost indestructible and will remain alive for a long time in burlap moistened with sea water. When dead, they may be kept in a strong brine solution, salty enough to float an egg. This is perhaps the only bluefish bait that works as well pickled as fresh.

Almost any small fish is suitable for taking blues whether fished alive, dead, whole or cut into chunks. With whole baits, remember that a bluefish usually strikes at the head of any natural swimmer less than six inches in length, but will chop anything larger than that into pieces by striking at its mid-section. Hooks should be placed with this fact in mind. If cut chunks are used, run the hook point through the fleshy side of the dorsal section rather than through the soft under-belly.

Some baits deteriorate much faster than others. Oily fish, such as menhaden and mullet, keep poorly unless well refrigerated. A bit of salt sprinkled over them will prolong their usefulness.

Hooking mummichogs (killies) can vary. Through the body when dead (top); behind dorsal fin (center) or through the lips (bottom) when alive. Photo by Hal Lyman.

Mullet are favorite baits in southern waters. Except for small finger mullet, the bait is usually cut in chunks. Photo by Vlad Evanoff.

Squid are in a class by themselves, for a squid that is turning pink will produce an aroma that makes your eyes smart. If they must be kept for any length of time, the best bet is to freeze them. Their flesh is tough and does not become mushy after thawing, which is a fault common to most bait fish.

Many anglers buy their bait at local coastal shops. For those who concentrate on chumming, commercial freezers furnish blocks of various species which may be thawed in a bucket of salt water, then cut up or ground. If you want to catch your own bait, a long-handled dip net, a cast net or small beach seine may be used. Concerning the last named, check local regulations. Some seashore communities have strict regulations on such seining.

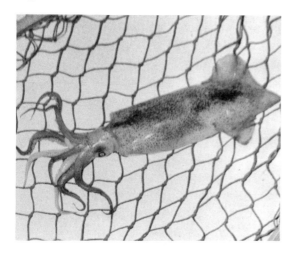

Squid is an extremely tough bait and may be used whole, chunked or cut in strips. Photo by Frank Woolner.

As noted, bluefish can be selective. A shrimp may do the trick one day and be worthless the next. Cut mullet might sweep the beach on Tuesday and be fit only for crabs on Wednesday. To discover just which bait works best at any point in time, a high-low rig, in which one hook is spaced about a foot above another, is a good device. Each hook can be baited with a different item until the proper combination is found. If limited to a single hook, present a bait cocktail—a chunk of herring tipped with a strip of squid, for example.

Any bait should be rigged to make it look as natural as possible. Even a cut chunk of mackerel may be given some additional appeal by moving it along the bottom with rod tip action. This was well illustrated by accident while I was fishing at Cape Hatteras, North Carolina. The surf line was crowded and anglers were using bait, so casting an artificial would only have made enemies. I lobbed a chunk of mullet seaward, waited for a few minutes, then noticed that my line was drifting towards a neighbor. I started a slow retrieve—and immediately had a strike! After beaching the bluefish, I tried the same system again, took another fish and then missed two more. My neighbors were talking to themselves. When I suggested they move their bait slowly, they hooked up and we were a happy trio until the tide changed.

A small float between the hook and sinker often will accomplish the same thing, for it will move the bait around slightly with the current. Some color such floats so that they will act as attractors in themselves. Tackle manufacturers are aware of this and several colored floats, such as the Fireball, are available at tackle shops.

Arguments among bait fishermen rage around whether or not the sinker should be rigged above the hook so that leader and bait trail from it to move naturally, or below it so that the slightest nibble may be felt, unhampered by the sinker's weight. Frankly, when still fishing for blues, I have never found that there is a great deal of difference as far as results are concerned. I often shoot for the best of all possible worlds by having one hook rigged above the sinker and another below it, a sort of variation of the high-low combination.

Live bait falls into a special category. Obviously the main purpose of using an active crab, alewife, or other sea creature is to make the offering appear as natural as possible—and alive! The hook therefore should not be driven through some vital part of the bait's anatomy. Sinkers or other weights must be kept to a minimum. If it is necessary to go deep, place the sinker between line and leader rather than close to the live bait itself—or use wire line. The bait will then be able to swim with as little restraint as possible.

LURES

When it comes to artificial lures, bluefishing history becomes fascinating. The so-called bone lure was a favorite back in the late 1800s and there was a sudden dearth of cats in Morehead City, North Carolina. A lucrative market was developed by boys who secured a dead cat—or converted a live one to a corpse—buried the critter for a while, dug up the remains, and then sold the shank bones in the angling market for 50 cents apiece.

These bones are hollow. Cut into pieces about three inches long, they were slipped over a long-shanked hook and a wire leader was placed in the hook eye. This leader was then twisted around a broomstick to form coils. When drawn through the water minus the broomstick, the lure trailed bubbles and, due to the leader coils, had an erractic motion that was irresistible to bluefish. The future of the Morehead City felines was secured when it was discovered that turkey, goose and chicken leg bones bleached in the sun worked equally well. Today, plastic tubes of various colors and surgical rubber tubing have been substitutes and members of the S.P.C.A. breath more easily.

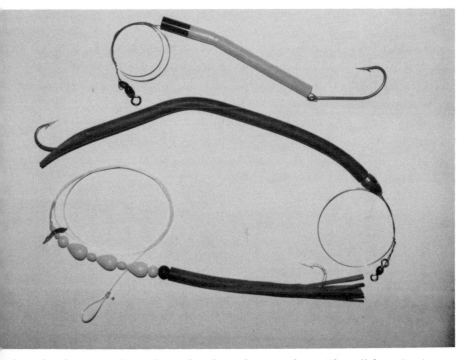

odern developments from the turkey bone lure: a plastic "bone" lure (top); sur-al tube (center); tube with beads and spinner (bottom). Photo by Hal Lyman.

Bluefish lures appear to go through cycles. Genio Scott had an illustration in *Fishing in American Waters* of a metal jig into which a piece of mother-of-pearl had been set. The lure disappeared for years, then surfaced again in the 1940s with shimmering plastic in place of the mother-of-pearl. After the death of the manufacturer, who was a small operator as far as production was concerned, again it vanished from the dealers' shelves. Then, in 1973, it once more reappeared with a design almost identical to that of Scott's sketch. After several more seasons, it was difficult to find, but today there are several lure models of similar design back on the market. And they still take fish!

Heave-and-haul handline fishermen tossed lead drails weighing a pound or more from the beach to take blues right up until the time when modern surf casting tackle was developed. This drail is the father of the metal jig or squid. Because lead tarnishes quickly in salt water, the lure had to be scrubbed with sand or scraped with a knife after a few casts to keep it bright. Some of these old heave-and-haulers, who coiled 100 yards of stout marlin pegged at one end in the sand at their feet, rubbed the lead with mercury, and the shine lasted. The next step was to make such lures of solid tin, and the name tinclad evolved. Now a wide variety of stainless steel and plated lures is available. Noteworthy among these are the Hopkins No-Eql lures of hammered stainless steel and the Acme Kastmaster, which is today's plated version of the old Eda Splune originally made from stainless. The Splune, incidentally, was one of the few lures for which the designer was able to obtain a patent.

Although tinclads are no longer made of tin because of the cost of that metal, any bluefisherman who casts has a wide variety of shapes and sizes in his tackle box. Many designs have evolved over the years and often have been labeled in accordance with their point of origin as is the case with the Montauk Squid and the Point Jude Wobbler.

An ancient metal lure, used for bluefish and many other species, is the diamond jig, a four-sided model tapered at each end. Its primary use is for fishing deep. Lowered close to the bottom, it is given action by raising and lowering the rod tip sharply or it

So-called tinclads or metal squids in all shapes and sizes for surf casting. Designs are streamlined to cut down on wind resistance. Photo by Hal Lyman.

may be retrieved in the same manner as a tinclad. However, the diamond moves basically through a vertical plane rather than a horizontal one. New England bluefishermen favor a treble hook on such jigs while those in the Middle Atlantic insist upon a single. The hook itself may be decorated with plastic tubing or even a strip of natural bait.

Cedar jigs with lead heads and wooden bodies were first used as bluefish trolling lures. A few are still available from those who craft them by hand. As tackle improved, it became obvious that these same cedar jigs could be cast. Salt water plugs, first developed by American Indians and then improved for taking seatrout in southern waters, might be considered to have cross-bred with the jigs. A whole new line of lures flooded the market after World War II.

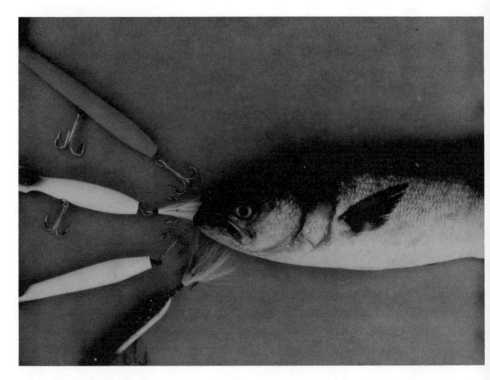

Bluefish will take plugs which appear much too large to fit in their mouths. Photo by Frank Woolner.

Plugs are American in origin and Americans enjoy fishing with them. When a bluefish explodes under a surface popper, the reason is clear to see. Even though I have had this happen to me countless times, I am still inclined to put tooth marks on my heart when the attack comes. Although poppers get the most spectacular results, never neglect the sub-surface models. These can be particularly effective in swift currents.

Because a plug is festooned with hooks, many believe that a bluefish will be taken more readily on it than on a jig with a single barb. Such is not necessarily the case. A blue can exert leverage against the plug body and tear itself free. In addition, one of its fellows is apt to take a cut at the lure visible in the hooked fish's jaws and part the line or leader. How they do it, I have never learned, but bluefish also can grab a plug, run with it for sufficient distance to take line off the reel against the drag, then spit the lure out to depart unscathed. I wish someone would take underwater photos of this phenomenon to determine just how the fish avoids the hooks.

To give a wooden plug or metal lure the appearance and perhaps the scent of natural bait, fish skins were secured to the lure's exterior in the early days. It soon became evident that the common eel produced the best skin for this purpose and eelskin-covered jigs and plugs followed, along with the metal eelskin rig itself. This lure has a weighted, hollow head. Water fills the skin tied around that head to make the whole works swim in a natural manner. Bluefish will hit all such offerings as well as whole rigged eels and plastic imitations. The difficulty is that the lure will be torn to pieces often after only one blue has been hooked.

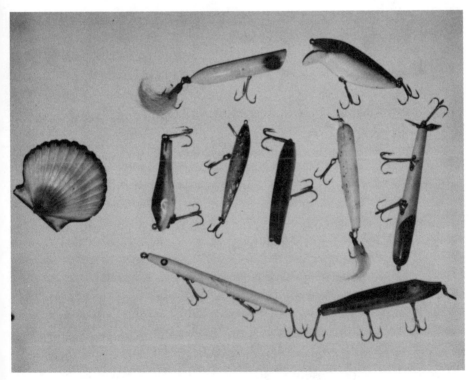

Design for bluefishing plugs vary widely from surface poppers through swimmers and darters and to deep running underwater models. Photo by Hal Lyman.

Trolling lures may vary from spoons (left and right), Japanese feather and artificial squid (center), to Accetta Mop (bottom). Photo by Hal Lyman.

An excellent bluefish lure—and one often forgotten by modern anglers, perhaps because it is identified primarily with fresh water use—is the spoon. I managed to keep this favorite secret weapon out of sight of rival bluefishermen for many seasons by tucking a couple of spoons into my pocket and leaving them out of the tackle box. Unfortunately for my reputation for bluefishing knowledge, others had long memories, too, and tried trolling spoons in the early 1970s. They worked. My secret weapon, which was really no secret at all, has become standard equipment for any serious bluefisherman. Good salt water spoons come in a wide variety of sizes and styles, which is a great advantage when trying to match the bait upon which the fish are feeding. They should be trolled more slowly than other lures for high speeds cause them to spin, thus twisting the line.

Another general lure type is among the ancients of the marine fishing world. The so-called Japanese feather consists of a weighted metal head through which a leader wire is passed and secured to the hook. The rear of the head is decorated with feathers, plastic, crimped nylon, or some other material. The generic name of Japanese feather is now applied to many trolling lures even though they may have no trace of Oriental origin and even less of feathers.

Similarly, the bucktail jig, also called leadhead, may be trimmed with all sorts of dressing other than bucktail. This is primarily a casting lure, yet it may be trolled or jigged in the depths. It features a weighted head so designed that the hook point rides upwards and therefore does not foul on the bottom. Lures collectively called "bucktails" are among the most commonly used of all artificials, for they often are employed in a

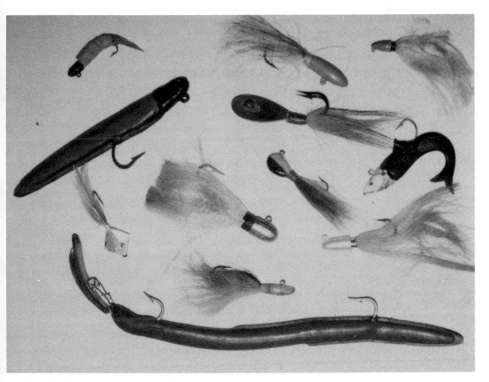

A shoal of casting lures for fishing deep. Trim may be feathers, bucktail, nylon or plastic. Photo by Hal Lyman.

mixed fishery where species other than bluefish are encountered. Like the true Japanese feathers, they tend to become thoroughly chewed and torn to bits by hungry blues.

A peculiar sort of lure was typified by the Tony Acetta Jig-It-Eel and the Ragmop made by the same manufacturer. Designed for trolling, their appearance will startle an inland trout fisherman to the point of numbness. The former is a lead-headed lure dressed with very long strands of straight or crimped nylon while the Ragmop features a light chain behind the head. Cross tied lengths of soft, wriggly nylon fiber are run through the chain links. Whether or not these lures look like a small school of bait is anyone's guess. They still catch fish, but have been replaced in most areas by a lure with a similar undulating action, the Hoochy Troll made by the Weber Tackle Company with plastic skirts of various colors. These and many imitations should be given additional fish appeal by sharply raising and lowering the rod tip while trolling.

A lure, if it can be graced with such a designation, which definitely does imitate a school of bait fish is the umbrella rig. It was the outgrowth of the old Chesapeake Bay "Christmas Tree," which is a single spreader from which three or more individual lures are trolled on short leaders. The umbrella features two such spreaders rigged at right angles to each other around a central hook. They catch a lot of bluefish and, because the many hooks slash and tear the flesh of fish that are never boated, injure many more. They can also impart wounds to the person trying to boat one or more blues hooked on the same rig. Strictly a meat fishing device, the umbrella is mentioned only because it is popular among some who want to fill the fish box. Sporting it is not!

Color in artificial lures can be important. More than a century ago, a physiologist by the name of Johannes von Purkinje was strolling through the countryside of what was later to become Czechoslovakia. He noted in the early morning that blue flowers appeared to be brighter in color than those that were red. After the sun started to decline, the reverse was true. His treatise on this phenomenon gave rise to what is now termed the Purkinje effect. Boiled down to fundamentals, this means that blue, silver and green are more visible to the human eye in morning light and red, yellow and gold take over as the sun declines. Experiments indicate that a fish follows the same general visual pattern. Knowledgeable bluefishermen profit by this fact when selecting lure colors.

In addition, when waters are murky or on overcast days, try a lure that is basically yellow. After dark, coal black lures can produce surprising results, particularly when the lure is on or near the surface. It is outlined against the lighter sky for a bluefish swimming under it. The area fished should also be taken into account. For example, red and white surface plugs can be very effective in Florida waters, yet do not produce well along the New England coast. In brief, if one color does not work, try another!

Every season, some particular lure will take the lead over all others. Anglers happily decide that the solution to all their problems has been found. When the next season rolls around, the killer of the year before may be almost worthless and it is forgotten. My memory for such things is good and I always try out effective lures of the past from time to time. Sometimes, as in the case of the spoon, I hit the jackpot. More often, I catch nothing, but like the Count of Monte Cristo, I wait and hope. There is always another year coming.

7

BOAT FISHING

From small skiffs to huge party boats, floating craft of one sort or another are utilized in the pursuit of bluefish. Unlike the shore angler, whose fishing horizons are limited geographically to a strip of water only about 150 yards seaward of tideline, the boatman has as his hunting grounds all the ocean that may be covered safely by the type of vessel employed. He may in truth pursue the fish.

In this connection, let me emphasize at the outset that some fishermen afloat pursue too eagerly. They rush from place to place at full throttle where blues are sighted or birds are working, then steam through the center of the school. It is possible to pick up a chopper or two when this is done, but the majority of the blues will scatter. The loom and shadow of the boat, with an assist from propeller noise right over their heads, will put them down. The craft should be maneuvered so that a cast or trolled lure passes along the school's edge. Fish chasers can ruin the chances not only for themselves, but also for any other anglers in the vicinity.

The type of boat selected by a bluefisherman depends upon many factors including personal taste, the type of waters usually fished and, perhaps most important of all, the angler's budget. A youngster after snappers in a sheltered bay may be reasonably content in a rowboat. His parents might choose a fiberglass hull

ical center console boat use for bluefishing along all sections of the Atlantic and f Coasts. Photo by Spider Andresen.

in the 20- to 30-foot length bracket with power enough to get to offshore rips in a hurry. An open cockpit is favored by most since it allows plenty of room for casting. For those who fish well offshore in rough waters, such as those found off the Race in Connecticut or at the edge of the Gulf Stream further south, larger cruisers are the rule. Trying to battle the elements in a craft too small to do so not only ruins the sport, but also can add to Coast Guard fatality statistics.

For those not owning their own boats, rental small craft liveries are studded along the coasts for inshore fishing. Charters also are available for offshore bluefishing and a small group can share expenses and sail when the spirit moves. Lower in the financial scale are the party boats, which leave the docks on a fixed schedule and charge a base fee per angler. Among blue-fishermen, they are especially popular in the Middle Atlantic coastal area.

STILL AND DRIFT FISHING

The fundamental method of angling from a boat is still fishing with the craft at anchor. This system dates back to prehistoric times when the first Waltonian caveman sank a gorge—nothing more than a stick sharpened at each end—into a hunk of bait, lowered it into the water, then waited for the fish to come to him. Actually the bait even in those bygone days was not "still" at all. Water moves around the offered meal as the currents flow. Today, the angler may impart movement to the hook and, at times, may cast bait and terminal tackle a considerable distance to reach the area where bluefish may be feeding.

Despite the simplicity of so-called still fishing, there are various refinements which should be noted to achieve maximum success. Remember always that bluefish are predators, not scavengers. If the bait is not alive, it should be very recently dead or in a good state of preservation through quick freezing. Various pickling solutions, such as brine, may keep bait fish flesh in good enough condition to take other species, but it does not work well for blues. As previously noted, rigged eels and eelskins are the exceptions.

Even when anchored, a boat will swing so that those fishing from the up-current side will find their lines rubbing against the hull. Under these circumstances, reel in, then "feel for bottom" again so that the line runs freely from the rod tip to the hook without abrasion. If no results come from fishing right on the ocean floor, try presenting the bait at lesser depths until blues are located. Slow jigging of the rod itself improves chances of success.

Drail and chain rig. The snap is passed through the jaw or eye socket of the bait fish and the hook is imbedded in the fish's flesh.

Besides still fishing, another more or less passive method of presenting natural bait to blues is drifting. From a boat, the angler allows his craft to move with the current and a baited hook moves along with it. Again, "feeling for bottom" is important since the hull will be passing over waters of varying depths. Drifting is not recommended in areas where currents are strong—often areas where bluefish are plentiful! It can also make instant enemies if many boats are fishing by other methods in any given part of the ocean. A drifting craft is basically out of control and thereby becomes a navigational hazard, particularly if someone aboard is fast to a fighting bluefish.

In gentle currents, when there is plenty of sea room, drifting can be amazingly successful in locating blues. In the early season, when the fish normally are deep, any type of natural bait may be bumped along just off the bottom. When there is a strike, have the anchor ready to be eased over the side without making a tremendous splash. A sinker should be rigged between line and leader so that the bait rides naturally. I choose lead-core or a short shot of wire line over any type of sinker for this method of fishing. Keep "feeling for bottom" by letting out line at regular intervals until you are sure that the hook is near the ocean floor, then reel in a foot or two. Sometimes terminal gear may be lost due to snagging, so this system is not recommended when fishing over very rough and rocky bottom.

When drifting, a whole bait or a strip cut from a fish—even from the belly of a bluefish—is better than a cross-section chunk. The fluttering action has particular appeal when drifted slowly. Pork rind may be substituted if natural bait is not available.

True artificials are also effective. The term "spin-jigging" was coined in Florida for a particular refinement of drift fishing. As the boat moves down-current, a cast is made with a bucktail type lure from the *up-current* side of the craft. The lure is then allowed to sink with a free line until it hits bottom. The retrieve is slow and the rod tip is lifted smartly after every two or three turns of the reel handle. This causes the lure to hop along close to the ocean floor. Blues at times will follow a jig presented in this manner right to the surface and will snatch it just a moment before it is lifted from the water. It therefore pays to fish every cast right to the end.

I use a modification of this system even when trolling. Frankly, I become bored with trolling after a time when action is slow. Then I may be found on the foredeck of the trolling vessel casting ahead and slightly to one side of the bow with a deep running lure. As the boat approaches the sinking hook, I reel in just enough to keep a tight line. Then, when the line is roughly abeam, I start jigging and reeling rapidly. Many times I have picked up bluefish which apparently have little interest in the trolled offerings.

Drift fishing is not confined to the bottom zone. If several anglers are aboard and blues have not been located, have each fisherman try a different depth during the drift. Once pay-off waters have been discovered, all can then shift to them. If trying one particular area, such as a known shoal, do not steam back up-current right through the good water. Give it a wide berth, circle, then kill the engine when in the proper position to start drifting again.

CHUMMING

Chumming for blues was developed to a fine art in the Middle Atlantic area a decade ago. Craft ranging from unsafe outboard skiffs of too small size for ocean work to large party boats with all modern safety equipment aboard studded the sea by day and night during the peak season. They anchored, then crewmen ladled chum over the side. The usual chum then, and also today, was ground menhaden, known locally as mossbunker, or simply bunker. The blues follow the chum slick to obtain a free meal. In times past, the quantities of chum were so great off the northern New Jersey shore that many gourmets claimed, with some truth, that bluefish taken from the area towards the end of the season acquired a definite taste of menhaden oil when prepared for the table.

Although chumming has declined in recent years and has become basically a night fishing method, it still is effective. A good chum slick is obtained by ladling small amount of ground fish or other enticer over the side at frequent intervals, not by dumping gobs of the stuff into the ocean every five minutes. Bait can be a piece of the chum itself. If finely ground, a half handful can be dropped into a piece of nylon stocking or milady's hairnet and then tied to the hook with fine thread. Be sure that milady does not want to use either the stocking or the hairnet ever again! For reasons best known to the bluefish, a bait of some totally different kind often will give better results, as will artificials. Although I have maintained previously that a whole bait is often better than a cut one, many anglers do very well with chunks of butterfish or menhaden when fishing in a chum slick.

Unless fishing from your own craft or with understanding friends, do not use very light tackle when chumming. One hooked blue that races around and about in the slick will spook others, and will also tangle every line within swimming range. Another way to court sudden death at sea is to run at high speed through another boat's chum line, or to anchor just down-current. Any angling judge will find for the defense under such circumstances. It may be considered justifiable homicide.

Some small boat anglers use a weighted burlap bag filled with chum to provide their own small, private slick. A screened box will do the same thing. Along some sections of the Gulf Coast, chumming at night around oil rigs is practiced with pieces of shrimp as bait and leavings from shrimp processing plants used as the chum itself.

Terminal tackle when using natural bait with this method can be specialized. To the line is attached a swivel, then about three feet of 40- to 50-pound test monofilament. Tied into the end of the mono is about a foot of leader wire, with or without a sinker between the two. At the wire's end of course is the hook. The purpose of the heavy mono is to swing the bluefish aboard, thus doing away with the need for a gaff or net.

One reason that the large chumming fleet of the Middle Atlantic area has been reduced is that party boat skippers have found that jigging with diamond jigs, mentioned in the chapter on lures, is highly effective on the same grounds. In addition, a rig that appears to defy all the rules of keeping a sinker well away from the hook has taken over. Known as the drail and chain, it employs a sinker tied to the leader, although often a leader is not required. At the lower end of that sinker, either a hook or a snap is secured, which is passed through the head of a whole bait fish. A short length of chain is added with a hook at its terminal end which is imbedded in the bait. Fished just off the bottom, this rig has great appeal for blues for reasons beyond my understanding. Party boat skippers are not stupid and the expense, nuisance and messiness of using quantities of chum can be eliminated to a large degree through use of diamond jigs and drail and chain rigs. They make the obvious choice while still providing blues for their clients.

One final point before leaving the subject of chumming. An artificial lure may be given added appeal when fishing in a slick by rubbing it in the chum. At this writing, many suppliers are also furnishing a wide variety of scents to be applied to lures for the same purpose. This trick is as old as cod liver oil. Just how effective these scents may be, I cannot guarantee, but they are certainly worth trying when bluefish are fussy.

TROLLING

Statistics are not available on the point, but my guess is that trolling is the most popular method for catching bluefish along all coasts. A newcomer to the ocean front is able to take his share of fish if he keeps the rod tip up and has the strength to reel. Basically, there are three primary factors to be considered when trolling: speed of the boat, depth of the lure or bait, and the lure or bait itself. They are all closely interrelated. An additional factor, which seems to bother neophytes more than it should, is the amount of line streamed from the reel. As I hope to explain in a moment, this varies. In brief, there should be enough line out to reach the fish!

Blues have been known to hit lures trolled at speeds in excess of 20 knots, but I do not recommend burning fuel at such a rate. On the average, speeds ranging between five and eight knots may be considered to be ideal under normal conditions. When fishing deep—that is, when the hook travels 50 feet or so below the surface—select a rate at the lower end of this range. Fast travel, when a heavily weighted terminal rig is being used, puts a tremendous strain upon line, rod, and even the angler. When the boat is slowed or stopped for the ensuing battle after the strike, chances are good that there will be slack line. Blues take full advantage of such slack and shake the hook.

Note that, when the boat is turned, lines streamed from the side towards which the turn is made will drop down deeper than normal while those on the other side will run closer to the surface. If the hook is **running** close to bottom, the first named lines should be reeled in slightly to prevent fouling bottom.

Boat speed should be varied to allow for current. For example, when trolling in a five knot current at a speed of five knots in the current's direction, the lure sinks and moves through the water with almost no action. Conversely, when trolling against the same current at the same speed, both boat and lure will be stationary with respect to the bottom while water will move around the lure at five knots. It is as though the boat were anchored, yet it may be maneuvered so that the hook covers a considerable amount of water as the boat is angled across the current. If there is a choice—and there usually is—troll against the current or across it at a slight angle, rather than with it.

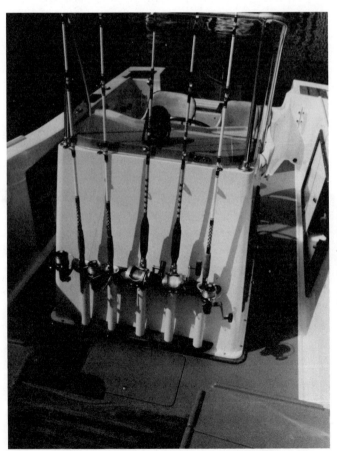

A battery of light tackle outfits for both trolling and casting for bluefish is standard equipment in inshore and offshore waters. Photo by Mako Marine.

Angling across a current in this manner can be developed into a fine art when fishing tide rips. Blues tend to hang in the area a few yards down-current from the visible surface of the tide rip itself. The boat should be a minimum of ten yards from the sighted rip and the angler should let out enough line so that his lure passes through the pay-off water. Experienced skippers can troll a rip in this manner within spitting distance of one another without collisions or line interference. When the end of the rip is reached, the boat concerned speeds up, heads up-current, then proceeds with lines reeled in to its original starting point to repeat its run. One of the quickest ways known to make bluefishing enemies is to turn down-current and steam through the edge of the rip, thus spooking every fish in the area.

Obviously current force will be directly related to the speed of trolling. When there is little or no current, the five to eight knot rate is recommended. If fishing near the surface, the lure should ride just beyond the second wave of the wake astern. Do not be afraid to vary the speed when there are few strikes or to vary the length of line streamed. There are exceptions to the rate recommended above. Although mullet are not known for their swiftness, blues feeding on them seem to prefer a fast moving lure, so jog the throttle up a notch when this bait is in the area. The same holds true when squid are providing the forage.

During the early season or at other times when blues are feeding at or near the bottom, slow down so that the hook travels only a foot or less over the ocean floor. Sinkers, wire, or lead-core line will take the lure down. In Connecticut's Race bluefishing grounds, anglers often combine wire line with a shiny sinker to get deep in a hurry. The sinker itself attracts fish to the lure, which trails astern on a two- to four-foot leader.

Downriggers are also useful when presenting a deep offering. The weighted downrigger line is attached to the actual fishing line with a snap release and the whole works is lowered to the desired depth. When a blue hits, the line to the rod comes free and the angler can fight the fish without the handicap of sinkers or wire. Even fly fishing tackle may be employed when this device is used.

Rarely is it necessary to stream dozens of yards of line when fishing at or near the surface. Blues generally are not line or leader shy in deep water. They may even be attracted to the wake of a boat to see what the commotion is all about. In shallow water, however, the wake may have the opposite effect and can spook fish for yards around. Therefore troll with a long line and at slow speed on the shoals or in shallow estuarine waters.

When bluefish schools are surfacing, then disappearing, chances are good that they will be back in the general area where they first surfaced. Keep trolling in the direction towards which the fish were moving when first sighted. A handful of chum to make a slick, a piece of crumpled paper, or even a teaspoonful of common dye will serve to help relocate the original spot where the fish were sighted. In these days of pollution awareness, avoid plastic markers.

If no strikes follow after a brief period, try what the U.S. Navy calls a retiring search plan. Simply head due north from the marker for 50 yards. Then turn east for another 50, thence south for 100, west for 150, north again for 200, and finally east once more until you get discouraged. You may also circle the spot in ever-increasing spirals, but the course changes at right angles are more easily controlled by the helmsman.

Since blues often do not cooperate by showing themselves,

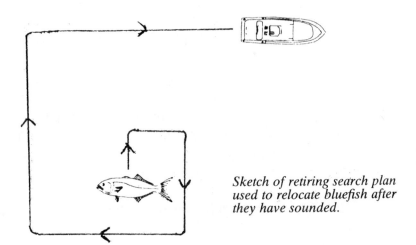

Sketch of retiring search plan used to relocate bluefish after they have sounded.

the troller must take his chances in known good areas such as tide rips or along the beach surf line. This last does not mean the point where waves are breaking, but where waves make up before they break. When close to shore, ranges may be taken on landmarks to relocate pay-off spots.

Modern electronic equipment has been a great boon to off-shore bluefishermen. Loran makes it possible to pinpoint prime feeding grounds. When marked on a navigational chart, such areas may then be revisited hours, or even weeks, later. In such recordings, note the stage of tide and direction of current when success was greatest since blues will shift their position when such factors change.

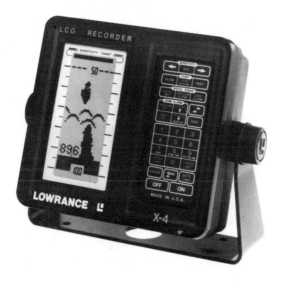

Highly sophisticated electronic equipment makes the boat angler's work easier. This model automatically sets its own ranges and sensitivity and provides a constant bottom reading. Photo by Lowrance Electronics.

The depth-sounder has become an almost indispensable piece of equipment for those who concentrate on boat fishing. With it, an angler can locate reefs and seamounts which, several decades ago, could only be found by careful piloting and manual soundings. Flickering dials and recording paper give a picture of the sea floor as a boat runs on any given course. This makes it possible to present a lure on the down-current side of some unseen underwater slope where the choppers lie waiting for tumbling bait.

Furthermore, on sophisticated dials or traces, you can spot the fish themselves and figure their precise depth. Those familiar with their equipment can even give an excellent estimate of the size of the blues swimming under the boat's keel. With experience, the tiny blips of light or marks on the recording roll can be translated to fish in the box.

Depth-sounders, which have been modified so that the sonar beam may be trained at all sorts of angles other than the perpendicular, now are available within a reasonable price range. These have the advantage of making it possible to scan a wide area underwater all around a boat. They are indeed fishfinders. Choice between portable and permanently installed equipment depends mainly on the size of the boat, with skiff and small boat operators naturally opting in general for portable gear. No matter what the choice, there is no question that a good depth-sounder is a basic weapon for the boatman.

Some bluefish trollers have gone back in history and do their fishing from sailboats, thus combining two sports in one. I have tried this method with Dr. John Homans of Brookline, Massachusetts, while fishing off the Block Island coast in Rhode Island. There is no question in my mind that a surfaced school of blues can be approached more closely in a sailboat than in a powerboat—and the school does not seem to be disturbed by the boat itself. When several hook-ups occur simultaneously in a brisk breeze, things can become a little frantic!

Before leaving the subject of trolling, let me say that my scant hair curls when I hear a bluefisherman say that he set the hook "again and again" after a strike. This is one of the best ways known to break up tackle and tear hooks from a fish's mouth. When you are trolling at high speeds, blues will set the hook themselves and usually will do so even at low speeds. This can best be illustrated by the fact that thousands of bluefish are hooked each year by unattended rods left in a rod holder. It is an instinctive reaction for any angler to lay back on the rod when a hit is felt, and no damage is done. Repeating the process serves no useful purpose and may well end in a lost fish.

CASTING FROM BOATS

After fish have been located by trolling, my choice is to kill the motor, drift or anchor, then go to work on the blues by casting. This system makes it possible to present a lure again and again to the quarry and normally gets better results than trolling alone. Be sure that you know your fellow anglers aboard and that you have control of your own casts. Once while fishing with an angler—who shall be nameless—off the Florida coast near Stuart, I had my cap removed three times in ten minutes by this character. I recommended in no uncertain terms that we start trolling. I do not want to be known along the coasts as Old One-Eye. Boat casting can be perfectly safe when those involved know what they are doing. It can be extremely hazardous when they do not.

Ideally when aboard small craft, a right-handed and left-handed fisherman can work without any interference. Such combinations are rare. Two right-handers should fish with the man in the bow casting to port and the man in the stern, to starboard. If both wish to cast to the same side, the bow man casting to starboard must be alert and careful; when both cast to port, the onus is on the stern man.

When a fish is hooked, it is polite to stop casting and allow the fortunate angler time to bring his catch alongside—polite, but not necessarily practical. Often blues will be moving fast so opportunities for hooking them are few and far between. In addition, several bluefish may follow their hooked companion and will strike readily at a lure presented close by. Here, accuracy and skill become important. If a plug or other lure is dropped near the blue trying to escape, an explosive strike often follows. Lines may cross and both fish be lost, yet this risk is worth taking, always providing that fishermen involved agree to such a procedure *before* leaving the dock.

Blues at times work into shallow water where a boat may not travel safely. Casting is the answer. By lying off in deep water, lures may be presented readily and the craft itself will not spook the fish. Obviously under such circumstances, the ability to

Casting from the bow of a moving boat, one of the author's favorite methods of taking blues. Photo by Spider Andresen.

Keeping hands away from a blue's teeth and from a plug's treble hooks is important when boating the fish. Photo by Barry Gibson.

throw a long line is an advantage. If fellow fishermen are on the beach casting seaward, move well out of range. Shorebound anglers have few choices among fishing areas while the boatman can cover a tremendous amount of water easily.

Once a school has sounded or disappeared, I prefer to stay in the same general area rather than to start trolling all over the ocean. Blues may travel fast, but bait schools normally move with the current. Drifting and casting at regular intervals off each side of the boat may relocate the feeding fish. If it does not, start the motor and move slowly, casting as before. When this fails, resume trolling at normal speed while using the retiring search plan described earlier.

If one technique of boat fishing fails, try another. Experimentation throughout the ages has brought new refinements to old methods and will continue to do so. Watch a successful bluefisherman and try to learn from him. I have followed my own advice for more than 60 years and I am still learning.

8

Shore Fishing

In the ranks of bluefishermen, the surf caster holds a place apart. Often bewhiskered and sleepless, always a little contemptuous of those who depend upon "stink pots" to reach their quarry, he feels that he combines the virtues of both hunter and fisherman. There is some truth in this attitude, for a surfman must have good knowledge of beaches, tides, currents, habits of bait and of bluefish themselves. Otherwise his quest may be unsuccessful. Confined to a limited area, when compared to the boatman, he must make the most of all opportunities.

Note, in my definition, that there is a difference between a surf fisherman in general and a surf *caster*. The former is one who fishes from the beach by any means, with natural bait or with artificial lures. The latter is more specialized: he casts and retrieves artificial lures only. Years ago in New Jersey, metal lures were termed "squids," even though they had little resemblance to the natural bait. "Squidding" and "squidder" have survived in the angling lexicon despite the fact that plugs are used widely today. A squidder therefore is a surf caster—and *vice versa*. Purists may claim that a true squidder uses a freespool reel, not a spinning reel, but I eschew this distinction.

Being able to read the water so that good spots may be distinguished from bad, and being able to cast accurately to a desired point, are the two prime requisites for a good surf caster. The ability to cast a long line comes in a poor third. Distance casting is a nice skill to have, of course. When blues are at extreme range, it means they can be reached. More important, when long distance casts have been mastered, shorter ones can be

Hal Lyman night fishing off Cape Cod beach when blues work inshore. Photo by *Frank* Woolner.

made with less effort and more accuracy. Those who specialize in trying to reach Spain with their lure all too often fail to fish the lure carefully right back to the beach edge. If they have a strike after half the line has been reeled in, they will claim that the bluefish followed the lure inshore. In point of fact, they may well be fishing beyond the point where the blues are lying and would improve their luck and save effort if they shortened their casts.

There is a distinct advantage in being able to cast more than 100 yards when the shoreline is crowded with anglers. A school of blues moving along a beach close inshore may become nervous when greeted by a shower of plastic, wood and metal lures, particularly when one or more of their numbers that hit such offerings disappear after being hooked. Added casting distance means that the lure falls in undisturbed water with a greater chance of a strike.

As is true when trolling, speed, depth and the lure itself are basic to success. Newcomers to surf casting worry a great deal, even as I did years ago, about the exact speed at which a lure should be retrieved. As a starting point with a standard free-spool reel, turn the handle about once a second when fishing with a metal jig. The rate should be lowered slightly when spinning since the ratio of handle to bail with such tackle is higher. Few have a stopwatch handy when surf casting, so count out loud: "One, chimpanzee, two, chimpanzee"—and so on. The interval will be about one second. Neighboring anglers may think you are a refugee from an animal farm, but ignore them.

When plug fishing, retrieve at a rate that will keep the line tight at all times. This is not difficult when using underwater or sub-surface lures. With surface poppers, it can present problems. The lure should be twitched with the rod tip to make it pop and, instantly afterwards, reeling should be speeded up to take in slack line. Some anglers—I am not among them—waggle their rods violently like a boy shaking a small apple tree throughout the retrieve to impart popping action. Without question, this method works, but I find it exhausting and, when there is a strike, both confusing and uncontrolled.

Charles Letson fights a bluefish in the surf. Note that the rod tip is held high to take full advantage of the rod's flexible power. Photo by Hal Lyman.

Normally when bluefishing, the lure should be moving towards the beach the moment it hits the water. This can be accomplished by lifting the rod tip as soon as the reel's gears are engaged or the bail is closed. If you are not waist deep in water or teetering on the edge of a rock jetty, a step backwards will help. There are exceptions to this general rule. If the blues are deep, it may be necessary to let a tinclad or bucktail sink down to their level. When the current is swift, blues may be caught by tightening the line, not retrieving at all, and jigging with the rod tip. Let the lure swing with the current until slack water is reached. Under crowded conditions, this method is not recommended because you will foul your neighbor's line.

This same system may be used to some degree with plugs.

Height is a help when scouting for bluefish from the beach although a beach roof not always handy. Photo by Frank Woolner.

With surface models, the exact target, such as a knuckle in a tide rip, may have been missed and the lure can be guided over it, then retrieved with suitable rod tip twitching.

Knuckles in tide rips—points where the currents clash in such a way that a small whirlpool or back eddy is formed—are prime bluefish producers. At times, it seems as though every blue in the county is lying in an area only a few square feet in size. Once on Monomoy Point on the southern spur of Cape Cod, Frank Woolner, Ted Lyman, the late Bim Simmonds and I were casting for blues shortly before sunset. Frank had been making disparaging remarks about the fighting ability of bluefish when compared to striped bass and their readiness to hit any and all offerings. We had covered the rip fairly thoroughly with no results when I dropped a jig into one particular knuckle. Immediately I was fast.

As I fought the fish and moved along the beach down-current to beach it, Ted stepped into the exact spot from which I had been casting, dropped his lure into the same knuckle, and also was fast. Bim followed suit, by which time my fish had been landed. I moved back into line before Frank realized what was going on. After the three of us had beached or lost a couple of fish apiece, we took pity on him and let him into the winner's circle. He cast to the knuckle, a fish was on, and the point was made that blues can be very particular indeed on just where they plan to dine. His attempts to horse the blue ashore failed and he was forced to admit that a bluefish fighting across a swift current can be a tough antagonist.

This also demonstrated that surf casters, working together, can fish a small area without interfering with one another. By timing casts carefully so that two lures are not in the air at the same time, or falling across a line that is already in the water, a number of anglers may fish practically shoulder to shoulder. Let one of them get out of cadence and the results are unhappy. The person who jams his way between two other fishermen on the beach and then casts like a windmill will soon find himself without friends.

In this connection, surf fishermen still fishing with natural bait and casters using artificials do not make a good mixture. The casters will continually foul the bait anglers' lines. If the majority are using bait, as is often the case in areas such as the Point at Cape Hatteras, North Carolina, and you favor artificials, move out of fouling range. Conversely, a bait fisherman who tosses a fish-finder rig out among a group of casters and thus denies access of others to a large chunk of ocean is as welcome as the proverbial picnic skunk.

When there are no other anglers in the neighborhood, remember to cast at various angles, not just straight out to sea. Often a blue will take a swipe at a lure moving nearly parallel to the breaker line when it will ignore one traveling a perpendicular path. This is particularly true if there is a strong current running along the shore. The lure moving *against* that current will get better results than one moving with it.

If a bluefish is seen to miss a lure or to hit without being hooked, there are two major avenues open to the surf caster— and to any other type of fisherman for that matter. The first is to drop the rod tip, give a little slack line, then start to retrieve again. The second is to jerk the lure forward, then reel like mad and give it all the action possible. In actual practice, I usually combine the two options. I drop the rod tip momentarily so that, if the fish has turned, it will have a chance to hit again where it first missed. Then I lift the tip smartly and reel rapidly.

Onshore winds, as noted, favor the beach fisherman, for they drive bait into the wash or close to it. However, such winds may make casting difficult. The trick is to cast as nearly into the wind as possible and, at the same time, keep the cast low so that a large belly does not form in the line. A speedy retrieve as soon as the lure hits the water will take up the slack. A strong cross wind is an anathema and there is no ideal solution for overcoming it. Low, short casts are the rule under such conditions, but even those result in a belly of slack line so that setting the hook on a strike is extremely difficult.

The surf caster uses tackle that is heavier than needed to beach a bluefish simply because it must be heavy enough to toss the lure into good water. As when trolling, the rule of *keep the fish coming* applies. If the fish jumps, old timers follow the rule of trying to break its neck—not literally, of course, but laying back on the rod to pull the fish off balance. Be prepared for a jump right in the wash when the bluefish feels sand under its belly. By dropping the rod to a horizontal position parallel to the beach itself, its bend will save many losses at this point in the battle.

When fish are breaking or sighted within casting range, drop the lure just ahead of the school if its direction of movement can be determined. In other cases, aim for the inshore edge. It is perfectly possible to hook a bluefish by casting beyond, or into the middle of, the flurry, but chances of taking another thereafter are reduced. The hooked battler will rush about among its companions and the line is apt to strike them, and thus alarm them, so that the whole school takes off for parts unknown.

Let me emphasize that there are no fixed rules concerning speed of retrieve, depth of lure, or type of lure itself. Be flexible. If one speed, depth or lure does not work, try another. Imagination and experimentation are just as important to a good surf caster as they are to a good research scientist. The same holds true for anglers using natural bait. If cut mullet is ignored, present whatever else may be available as a choice.

Casting from shore is not limited to the high surf by any means. There are times when bluefish in a feeding frenzy come right into the wash and even strand themselves. In 1971, for example, along the Outer Banks of North Carolina, beach walkers gathered in an amazing number of blues without benefit of hook, line, rod or reel. In their gluttony, the fish would beach themselves pursuing frantic bait on an incoming wave. As the wave receded, all that was required to collect an evening meal for the people on hand was a gentle kick that sent the bluefish flopping above high tide mark. Although unusual, such occurrences are not uncommon. When the fish are that close to shore, light tackle buffs, including fly fishermen, can profit.

Blues are attracted inshore by bait. If the bait is beyond casting range, the angler must go out to meet it. Such a system has been developed to a fine art along many sections of the coast, particularly in the New Jersey area. I do not mean that Jersey bluefishermen have acquired such divine qualities that they can walk on water: they simply clamber out on one of the many jetties that stud that coast. Marine growth covers such jetties, currents and eddies suck around them, bait fish gather—and the blues follow.

Sliding a blue onto the beach. Note that the rod is not held upright to minimize strain. Photo by Spider Andresen.

Jetty jockeys basically have become highly specialized surf casters. This method of fishing is not a game for the old and feeble, nor for those who have a poor sense of balance. Tackle is lighter than that used in the high surf, yet even such tackle is hard to handle when perched atop a slimy chunk of granite which may be ankle deep in water at one moment and waist deep the next. Metal hobnails or creepers on wader soles are part of the uniform of the day—or night. The trick is to get out on the jetty at the proper tide and, even more important, to get back before the tide rises to cut you off from dry land.

In general, the basics that apply to all surf casting apply also to jetty fishing. However, long casts as a rule are not needed. At night especially, bluefish may appear literally at your feet. On one occasion in the Point Pleasant area of New Jersey, I learned this the hard way. I had just decided that a chunk of rock a few yards along the jetty looked more enticing than the one I was standing on. Doing a balancing act, I extended my jetty rod parallel to the water to serve in much the same way as a tightrope walker's pole does for balance. Incidentally, this is a good procedure under normal circumstances even when wading, for the rod slapped down on the water surface can restore human equilibrium.

Foolishly, I had not secured the plug I was using. It dropped into the suds close to the jetty and a bluefish, which disliked me, grabbed it. The yank of the strike tumbled me head over heels in the middle of a stride. I saved the tackle. I saved myself. I did not save the fish. For some time afterwards, my thoughts were on my bruises and were far away from bluefishing!

That lesson has never been forgotten, even though the scars have healed. If it happened to me today, I might well not be writing this book, since my bones are more brittle than they were in my youth and I do not bounce readily off granite. At any rate, when I cast from a jetty, I fish the lure right up to my feet.

Since bait fish tend to work close inshore after dark when winged predators do not bother them, and since many of the groined beaches along our coasts are peopled with swimmers during the day, jetty jockeys are inclined to be people of the night. Standard equipment therefore includes a headlamp or some similar lighting device. Usually it is worn not on the head, but around the neck or waist and turned on only briefly when the beam is required. The reason: a wobbling ray of light stabbing through the darkness may scare bluefish away. Blues are not normally alarmed by navigational lights, such as those found on buoys, which remain in one place. They can be spooked by erratic flashes; therefore shield any light well and use it sparingly. A pencil flashlight held in the teeth serves well on the open beach when changing lures. I have never tried it on a jetty because I am afraid I might swallow it!

Casting, of course, is not limited to open beaches and jetties as a method of taking bluefish. Any platform, whether it be a pier, bridge, tidal river bank or sand bar will serve. From man-made structures, casting may be severely limited due to the presence of many other fishermen. On many fishing piers, overhand or side casting is strictly prohibited as a very sound safety measure. Those who have mastered the underhand flip cast will be winners. This cast is not difficult once the angler realizes that the snap of the rod does the work.

With a short drop-off between the rod tip and lure, bring the rod smartly forward as it points towards the water using wrist action primarily. Then snap it back so that the rod is fully flexed. Another snap forward as the line is released will send the lure or bait on a path approximately parallel to the water. The distance achieved is not great, yet it is often sufficient to place the hook where a blue will grab it.

Those fishing off structures over the water have a special problem after the bluefish has been played to exhaustion. The angler is separated from his catch by a large expanse of open air below his feet. Small fish can be derricked up to land level provided the tackle will take the strain. With larger specimens, there are two alternatives. The first is to lead the fish to the end of the pier or bridge and then beach it in the shallows. This is often impossible and is always a nuisance. The second is to have a very long-handled gaff or net, or to have a weighted snatchhook or net which may be lowered on a rope to lift the catch to safety. Most commercial fishing piers have such devices available. For the angler who makes a business of pier and bridge fishing, the snatch-hook is the easiest rig to carry. A treble-hooked cod jig tied to a length of stout cord serves the purpose well.

Light tackle casting from shore is both effective and good sport. More limited as far as maneuverability is concerned than his boating counterpart, the beach-bound angler may still cover a great deal of fish-holding water. Local knowledge is a prime ingredient for success. For example, a point on the seaward side of a tidal marsh may be little more than a mudflat at low tide, yet will be a prime bluefish feeding ground an hour before the top of the flood. Familiarity with holes and drops along an estuarine sod bank and the stages of tide when bait is carried into them leads to success. As is true in the case of a surf fisherman reading the beach, studying any coastal area at dead low tide is the best time to make actual or mental notes of prime grounds.

When winds and seas rage along the open coast, almost always there is some sheltered nook to be found in the lee of what is termed inside waters—bays, estuaries and tidal rivers. Here the light tackle angler comes into his own. Because he is working at closer quarters than his surf fishing contemporary, he must take greater care both in approach and presentation. Stamping heavily on the bank, allowing body shadow to fall across the nearby water where fish may lie, or splashing a huge lure onto a smooth water surface will spook the quarry. The angler must equate himself with a stalker.

Because underwater—and even above water—obstructions are particular hazards to light lines, it is always wise to follow the lead of bank burglars: case the joint before going into action. Make a mental note of just where the hazards lie so that, when a fish is hooked, you know when to put maximum pressure on it to prevent a cut-off. Also pick out for future reference a point along the bank or beach where the catch may be landed without too much trouble. Trying to reach a convenient little slope of sand, with an eight-pound bluefish leaping about on the

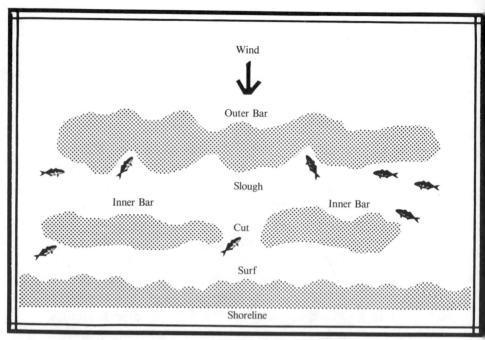

Typical beach structure with spots where bluefish lie when there is an onshore wind or current indicated. Current running from right to left or left to right in the slough between inner and outer bars bring bait inshore and the fish tend to gather in area facing the current. Any cut between two bars on either incoming or outgoing tide provides prime bluefishing waters.

end of an eight-pound line, can be frustrating if an eight-foot deep mudhole lies between you and the landing point.

On the first run when a blue is hooked on light tackle, it pays to copy the bonefisherman who wades the flats. Hold the rod well above your head so that the line runs well clear of the bottom. The slightest touch against a stick, rock or bit of shell when line is scorching off the reel spells disaster. I have reeled in slack without the comforting resistance of a fish or lure many times in such fishing, and undoubtedly will do so many times more. On each occasion, I try to analyze just what I did that was wrong and often find I have only myself to blame. Sometimes I have to come to the conclusion that the bluefish simply was smarter than I was!

In light tackle casting, play each and every current variation to the fullest extent. It takes little effort to repeat a cast several times until the lure lands in exactly the right spot. As in jetty fishing, work the lure right up to your feet, for a strike may come just as the hook is being lifted clear of the water. If the fish can be seen approaching when this is about to happen, you must have nerves of steel to resist an impulse to tweak the hook out of that slashing mouth. My nerves have yet to reach that stoic point—and I hope they never will.

Shore-based anglers cannot drift as a boatman does, but they can make use of a current to do the job for them. From the bank of a tidal river or estuary, from a bridge or pier, a bait, with or without weight added, is dropped into the water and allowed to move with that water while line is let out. When the desired section has been covered, the offering is then reeled back slowly with action given to it by twitching the rod tip. When no sinker is used, this method of fishing is known as live-lining. Note that, as the bait is being drifted down-current, the line should always be kept taut. Blues may hit at any time, and a great loop of line swinging loosely will result in a missed strike. As is true when drift fishing from a boat, artificial lures as well as live and dead natural baits may be employed. Natural bait chunks are not recommended, but strip baits work well.

Shore fishing methods are not stereotyped. Those writing about such fishing tend to place these methods in categories, just as I have done. In actual angling practice, there is a great deal of overlap. An experienced fly fisherman almost instinctively casts his lure across a current and lets that current give the lure action and speed on the retrieve. A surf caster, fishing a deep-running bucktail, does the same. The spin fisherman lets Nature provide a chum line on the outgoing tide at the mouth of an estuarine river. By watching the techniques used by those who take more bluefish than you do, then copying them, you will soon become one of the watched rather than a watcher.

9

The Leavings

As is true whenever I have almost completed a book, I find myself faced with a small heap of scribbled notes which I either forgot to fit into the proper chapter or simply felt that they did not fit well. Scientists, when preparing papers, have a neat trick under these circumstances. They end their presentations with a section entitled "Conclusions" in which everything is wrapped up neatly and the desk is cleared. What follows are not conclusions, but the leavings from material gathered over time.

First, considering the bluefish itself, never forget that it is a voracious feeder and, as such, has incredibly strong digestive juices in its stomach. Left uncleaned without refrigeration for any length of time, it will literally digest itself. The entire body cavity contents will spoil in short order and the flesh will be tainted. Clean your catch as soon as possible.

On large sport fishing craft, an ice-filled fish box is standard equipment. On smaller boats, portable ice boxes serve well in keeping the catch cool. Lacking such conveniences, a burlap bag which has been well moistened with sea water does a satisfactory job. Evaporation chills the contents, so keep the sack wet and out of the sun at all times. The beach fisherman may not even have a bag available. He can limit the ravages caused by hot sunlight by using a fish stringer to hold the catch in the water or by burying, temporarily, the whole fish in the sand. Never fail to

A beach buggy tailgate serves to keep a bluefish clear of the sandy beach while it is being filleted. Photo by Hal Lyman.

mark the interment spot with a piece of driftwood or stone. Digging about like a dog seeking a buried bone can be the height of frustration.

If cleaning a blue on a sand beach, do the job on a piece of plank or similar clean surface. Sand grains otherwise will work their way into the flesh, which may help your local dentist's bank account at a later date, but may discourage the gourmet. Resident seagulls will welcome the blue's entrails, but bluefish heads and skeletons should be buried deep or taken off the beach for disposal.

This is not a cookbook, so I do not intend to list all sorts of bluefish recipes. Cookbook authors do not tell me what tackle to use: I therefore stay clear of their area of endeavor in grateful acknowledgement of their forebearance in mine. However, it should be made clear that a bluefish filet spanking fresh makes a far better meal than one which has been lying around on ice for a long period of time. If the catch must be frozen, use the quick-freeze process, or place it in a container of slightly salted water prior to putting it in a home freezer.

This brings up the subject of salt water itself. In large quantities, as in the case of oceans, I find it extremely pleasant. In small, cold quantities, as in the case of leaking waders, it is the reverse. Charley Waterman of DeLand, Florida, who catches a good many fish in the course of a year and writes well about the catching, dons newly bought waders, then sits down in a bathtub full of water to browse through the evening paper. If there are any leaks, he discovers them under conditions that are comfortable and in a situation where he can make repairs easily. I have more faith in manufacturers than Charley does, but I do use this system to check out my waders at the opening of the fishing season after winter storage.

When storing waders for a long period of time, wash them thoroughly, both inside and out, with fresh water. Then hang them to dry. Manufacturers today urge that fishermen then store the waders in a plastic bag placed in a box that excludes all light. The reason: ozone attacks rubber and the tight storage cuts down on the amount of ozone reaching the waders' surface. Undoubtedly they have a point, but I do not think that many of those who give this advice live near the seashore. It is almost impossible for those of us who have our homes subject to ocean breezes to get waders completely dry inside and out. When stored tightly, they develop molds that would make a cheese-maker happy, but do more damage than ozone. I therefore opt for hanging them in a cool, dark spot.

Unless the weather is warm, when bathing trunks may be worn unless the sun is punishing, waders are the choice of the surf caster. With a foul weather parka belted at the waist, an angler so equipped is almost watertight. Hip boots are adequate for sod bank and estuary fishing. Ankle or knee boot models serve the boatman well and those with gripping soles, such as the Topsider line, should be favored.

A long-billed cap, known to the trade as a Block Island swordfisherman's cap, is my choice for headgear. The visor keeps sun out of the eyes and the cap fits snugly even when the wind is brisk. Frank Woolner favors a beret when winds howl and he is welcome to his choice. When I wear a beret, I feel that something is nesting in my hair. Under savage sun, a hat with a wide brim is advisable to keep sunlight from crisping the top of your ears. A length of line with a snap at each end—one snap for the hat and the other for a shirt's buttonhole—will prevent the hat from blowing out of reach. Many eschew my choice of headgear and select the visored baseball type of cap in its stead, but I guess I am a creature of habit and stick to what I have found best.

As for the remainder of my fishing garb, I pick a long-sleeved shirt because the sleeves may be rolled down when the sun burns. Light-weight long trousers are chosen for the same reason even when wading in midsummer. Full length jumpsuits are considered uniform of the fishing day in many southern areas. My objection to such a garment is that a bit of bluefish blood, mullet entrails or other unpleasant decoration means that the whole works must be tossed into the washing machine—and often a washing machine is not handy.

Shoes, other than waders or boots, should be of the deck-gripping type for the boatmen. These same models on a sand beach will become clogged and slippery: therefore choose crepe or solid rubber sole types ashore. I wear socks, not because I aim to qualify as the best dressed angler, but because they prevent sunburned ankles and also minimize friction between flesh and shoe when grains of sand intervene.

Polarized sun glasses should be standard equipment. Not only will they shield eyes from the sun's glare, but also they will enable you to spot fish lying below the surface. A short piece of line taped to the end of each bow and draped around the neck will keep them from slipping into the water. A neat rig for sun glasses, or corrective ones, for this purpose may be made by wrapping monofilament leader material around a nail, then securing the ends with tape and boiling the whole works in water for about ten minutes. After cooling, the mono will be in the form of a spring and may be taped onto the bows in the same manner as plain line.

Carrying extra lures and tackle replacements presents no problem to the bluefisherman who uses large boats or a beach buggy for his sport. The small craft angler is limited to some degree, but can stow a good deal of gear in a regular salt water tackle box. For stowage of extra clothing, I recommend the waterproof ditty bags which may be purchased in any war surplus shop. A tackle box located at the base of operations for the beach angler is all very well, but is a nuisance when covering a considerable stretch of beach.

A plastic bucket under these conditions serves the bait fisherman well and, with a cover on it, may also be used as a seat. Lures, hooks and leaders may be hung around the inside edge. For lures alone, many use a shoulder bag. However, when wading deep, waves toss it around at awkward times. Carriers that fasten to a belt around the waist are better. Fortunately several good models are now on the market—a fact that was not true a decade ago.

I do not use a gaff when surf casting. When fishing jetties, a belt gaff that doubles as a billy club does the trick. A billy club alone is useful both on the beach and afloat. An excellent way to lose fingers is to remove a plug from the snapping jaws of a bluefish which is still very much alive. Conk the fish on the side of the head and you will then be able to proceed without injury. Creasing a blue right across the top of the skull does not seem to bother it very much, for the skull bone is heavy.

Nets to render bluefish to possession from boats and shore structures may suffer considerable damage from teeth of bluefish. Metal mesh helps, but even with metal, the blue should be extracted from the mesh as quickly as possible. Net or gaff han-

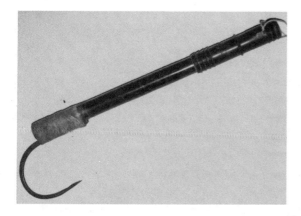

A simple belt gaff may be made from a tuna hook with the barb filed off and wrapped to a plastic or wooden shaft.
Photo by Hal Lyman.

dles should be long enough to reach well below the water surface so that the person using them does not have to bend over with his head below his heels.

If it were possible, I would have all those who plan to net or gaff bluefish train with a pier net on a rope or with a snatchhook. If this were done, it would become apparent to the trainee that the catch must be led over the retrieving device. Neophytes are apt to lash about like a butterfly collector in attempts to run the bluefish down. The terms "brought to net" or "brought to gaff" mean just that—and it is up to the angler to do the bringing.

A good stainless steel knife is part of the standard equipment carried by any bluefisherman. Those with blades which fold into the handle may be handy to stow in a pocket, but wet fingernails become soft so that it is difficult to bring the blade into action. A sheath knife should be the rule. Many sheaths also have a place for cutting pliers, another bit of needed equipment. The cutting jaws should be strong enough to sever a hook that may have become lodged in a place where it does not belong. When releasing blues, pliers are indispensable and the long-nosed models can help remove hooks taken deep.

Other incidental equipment should include a good pair of binoculars, sun screen lotion, insect repellant and a couple of Band Aids for minor injuries. My many medical friends tell me that amateur first aid treatment often causes more trouble than the original injury. I respect their opinion and recommend heading

A long-handled gaff makes boating a bluefish comparatively easy, although some what frantic. Photo by Barry Gibson.

for the nearest doctor in case of serious trouble.

As far as first aid for tackle is concerned, I always carry a spare rod tiptop of fairly large diameter. The tip itself may be built up to accomodate it with thread or fishing line. Ferrule cement, which melts when a match is applied, will secure it in place. Rod guides may be fashioned out of heavy leader wire in an emergency and then secured in place with electrician's tape. This tape has many uses and should be in every tackle box or bag. Add a bottle of nail polish for touching up frayed rod windings or damaged lures. Colored polish is also useful for marking wire line so that the amount streamed may be determined at a glance.

Salt water corrodes metal quickly, so it is wise to wash down all tackle with a fresh water hose after use. A small can of light oil plus another of the modern water-displacing lubricants, such as WD-40, CRS, and Systems-5 can save the day when reels or motors get balky.

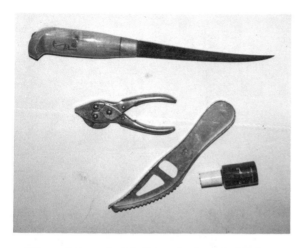

Basic equipment includes a good filleting knife, cutting pliers, fish scaler and nail polish. Photo by Hal Lyman.

The advice of old Captain Josiah Nickerson of Cape Cod, now long dead, was: "Keep feathers clean, metal bright and hooks sharp." That advice is as good today as it was years ago.

Whether it was the good Captain's ancestor or not, I do not know, but there is an apocryphal tale concerning another Nickerson which will underline my final point. Trolling from his catboat with a handline and a lead drail, he felt a tremendous strike, then the line went slack. Upon hauling in the lure, he found it bitten cleanly in two. Three days later on the same grounds, he caught a huge bluefish. When the catch was cleaned, sure enough, there was the tail end of the drail lodged in the fish's stomach!

The point, of course, is that bluefish have sharp teeth and will use them. I have noted this before, and will emphasize the fact in conclusion, in the hope that the fingers you save will be your own.

As long as blues continue to use those teeth, to attack a lure or bait with unequalled savagery, to battle spectacularly for their freedom, to upset all the rules of behavior just when you think you have learned something about them, I hope to be able to totter to the edge of the sea in my quest for bluefish until I pass over the River Styx.

Who knows? There may be bluefish in the Styx itself. Then, when Charon leans on his oars, I will have one last chance for glory!

Index

151